JIM CROW COMES TO CHURCH

*This is a volume in the
Arno Press collection*

THE AMERICAN CATHOLIC TRADITION

Advisory Editor
Jay P. Dolan

Editorial Board
Paul Messbarger
Michael Novak

*See last pages of this volume
for a complete list of titles.*

JIM CROW COMES TO CHURCH

Dolores Egger Labbé

ARNO PRESS
A New York Times Company
New York • 1978

Editorial Supervision: JOSEPH CELLINI

Reprint Edition 1978 by Arno Press Inc.

Copyright © by the University of
   Southwestern Louisiana

Reprinted by permission of the Center for Louisiana
   Studies, The University of Southwestern
   Louisiana

Reprinted from a copy in the State Historical
   Society of Wisconsin Library
THE AMERICAN CATHOLIC TRADITION
ISBN for complete set: 0-405-10810-9
See last pages of this volume for titles.

Manufactured in the United States of America

Library of Congress Cataloging in Publication Data

Labbé, Dolores Egger.
   Jim Crow comes to church.

   (The American Catholic tradition)
   Reprint of the 2d ed. published in 1971 by the
University of Southwestern Louisiana, Lafayette, which
was issued as no. 4 of USL history series.
   Bibliography: p.
   1. Church and race relations--Louisiana. 2. Catholic
Church in Louisiana. I. Title. II. Series.
III. Series: Louisiana. University of Southwestern
Louisiana, Lafayette. The U.S.L. history series , no. 4.
[BX1415.L9L3   1978]   261.8'34'51960730763   77-11295
ISBN 0-405-10838-9

JIM CROW COMES TO CHURCH

The Establishment of
Segregated Catholic Parishes
in South Louisiana

By

Dolores Egger Labbé

Second Edition

Copyright by
University of Southwestern Louisiana
Lafayette, Louisiana
1971

ACKNOWLEDGEMENTS

In preparing this work, both as a Master's thesis and for publication, I have had the invaluable guidance of Robert R. Jones.

Others have also given me great assistance. Father Peter E. Hogan, S.S.J., Josephite Archivist, searched the Josephite Archives for materials pertaining to the early black parishes. Archdiocesan officials made the study possible by permitting me free access to the New Orleans Archdiocesan Archives. A number of older residents of the area, both black and white, provided helpful information about Church life in South Louisiana in the early 1900's.

I am particularly grateful to Ronald M. Labbé for his criticism, proofreading, and editing, and especially, for his patience.

FOR DAD AND MOM
Raymond and Josephine Egger

TABLE OF CONTENTS

Introduction 1

I   Black Catholics and Their Church: The Ante-Bellum Years 8

II   Factors Maintaining Integration of Parishes in the Postwar Years 17

III   The Decision to Experiment 27

IV   Janssens' Experiment 42

V   The Experiment Becomes Permanent 63

Epilogue 85

Appendix 92

Bibliography 95

Index 100

JIM CROW COMES TO CHURCH

INTRODUCTION

After the Civil War most Southern Negroes who were Church members belonged to Protestant churches, and general statements made by Southern historians about Negroes and religion are applicable mainly to Protestant denominations.[1] Understandably the Catholic Church has received little attention. In most of the South it was a minor denomination containing few black members. Yet, the Southern historian cannot neglect the relations of black Catholics with their Church.[2] In South Louisiana, in particular, the Catholic Church has traditionally had many black members and in its ministry among them the Church has contributed to cultural patterns of life in the South. Our understanding of the extent and nature of this contribution necessarily involves an increasing knowledge of the historical position of blacks in the Catholic Church, and it is hoped that this study will make a contribution to this neglected body of knowledge.

An examination of the relations between the Church and its black members, in an area of the South populated predominantly by Catholics, reveals that the usual historical generalizations often do not apply to the Catholic Church. The thesis of this study is that the

---

[1]Many of the generalizations are found in the following books, Francis Butler Simkins, <u>A History of the South</u> (New York, 1953) and John Samuel Ezell, <u>The South since 1865</u> (New York, 1963).

[2]Throughout this study the Catholic Church will usually be referred to simply as "the Church."

Church in the Archdiocese of New Orleans[1] did not relate with its black members in the same way as Southern Protestant churches. It is true that both Catholic and Protestants eventually organized segregated churches, but they did so in a different manner, for different reasons. Catholics in South Louisiana never established completely separate church organizations and they did not introduce seperate church parishes until the 1890's, many years after Protestant churches had done so. Moreover, the first requests for separate Catholic churches did not come from Negroes as they had in the Protestant churches.

During Reconstruction most Southern Protestant churches approved separate congregations for blacks. They were usually willing to supply pastors and financial aid to them. Whites did not want Negroes to form independent associations, however, for they intended to keep them under white supervisions. Negroes, sometimes encouraged by Northern churchmen, demanded complete separation because paternal guidance in church matters did not appeal to them. They realized that their church was one institution in society which they could control completely and they were eager to establish associations of their own. Gradually, most Protestant denominations met the demands, splitting into separate organizations. In the new associations all positions of honor and leadership were held by Negroes. Any devout member of a congregation could serve as a minister in most churches as oratorical ability was more important than theological knowledge. Any small building, sometimes purchased with the assistance

---

[1] The Archdiocese of New Orleans in this study includes all of Louisiana south of the 31st degree of latitude. The reader must be careful not to confuse the city, which was not predominately Catholic, with the diocese, which was. The archdiocese was the only heavily Catholic area of the South. It was also the only diocese in the country with a very large black membership.

of whites, served as a church. At the services, which consisted of whatever forms and rituals the congregation desired, no one was forced to sit in a balcony or a back pew. Both blacks and whites appeared pleased with the success of the new arrangement.[1]

The Catholic Church could not allow the kind of separation permitted by her sister churches because of differences in church structure. Complete separation of races into independent and autonomous organizations is impossible, for according to canon law all Catholics within the geographical boundaries of a diocese are subject to the jurisdiction of the same bishop. Separate congregations, however, are possible. Nevertheless, only the bishop decides where and when new congregations will be formed and he has full authority in the appointment of pastors. His choice is limited, however, to formally ordained priests with seminary training. Unlike Protestant denominations the Catholic Church in South Louisiana continued to have integrated congregations during Reconstruction. Except for an occasional chapel,[2] all churches remained integrated until 1895; that year a black parish was created in New Orleans. It was a voluntary parish, and no Negroes were compelled to attend it. By 1900 missionaries were recruited to work exclusively with blacks in

---

[1] Walter L. Fleming, Civil War and Reconstruction in Alabama (New York, 1905), pp. 644-645; John Hope Franklin, From Slavery to Freedom: A History of American Negroes (New York, 1947), pp. 305-306; Simkins, History of the South, pp. 305-307; William Warren Sweet, Methodism in American History (Nashville, 1961), pp. 312-313; Carter G. Woodson, The History of the Negro Church (Washington, 1921), pp. 189-201.

[2] Roger Baudier, The Catholic Church In Louisiana (New Orleans, 1939), p. 421. Before the Civil War the free Negroes at Bois Mallet had a chapel which was served from Opelousas. There were several other chapels but no parishes.

two rural areas of the archdiocese, and several years later segregated parishes were established rapidly in many parts of the archdiocese. By 1918, when the new diocese of Lafayette was founded in Southwest Louisiana,[1] segregated parishes were considered both normal and permanent, and Negro Catholics were expected to attend them.

One of the main objectives of this study is to examine the activities and attitudes of the official and non-official Church[2] in South Louisiana in an effort to understand why black parishes were not begun before 1895, and to discover why they were considered a solution to the problematic relations of the Church with its Negro members by 1918. A second objective will be an attempt to explain how the Church, with its rather rigid structural requirements, was able to work out the details of segregated parishes. This will be done by an examination of most of the early parishes, built before 1918, and of the work of the several religious orders connected with them.

Just as many Southerners assume that Jim Crow laws have "always" existed in Louisiana, so, too, many Catholics in South Louisiana believe that segregated parishes are a part of a long-established Church policy. Both of these beliefs are inaccurate. Jim Crow laws were not enacted in Louisiana until the 1890's and segregated parishes in South Louisiana stem from the same period.[3] The development of these parishes has

---

[1] The new diocese was split off from New Orleans and included the area of South Louisiana west of the Atchafalaya River.

[2] The word "official" refers to the hierarchy, chancery officials and other members of the clergy. "Non-official" includes all other members of the Church. These adjectives will be used when needed for clarity.

[3] Henry C. Dethloff and Robert R. Jones, "Race Relations in Louisiana, 1877-1898," Louisiana History, IX (Fall 1968), 301-323.

received almost no attention from the scholarly community. A pamphlet, "For Men of Goodwill," written by Father Robert Guste of the New Orleans archdiocese, in 1957, gives some attention to the history of separate parishes, but, apart from that, they have been neglected.

The reader will notice that the study is concerned with the introduction of segregation into parishes, other institutions under Church jurisdiction being purposely avoided.[1] The rather ambiguous word "parish" requires an explanation, which is best given by canon law:

> The territory of every diocese is to be divided into distinct territorial units; and each unit is to have a special church with a designated people, and a special rector is to be given charge over it as its proper pastor for the necessary care of souls. . . . Such units are parishes.[2]

Since 1919 parishes have had to contain a permanent rectory for the pastor, and enough income must be available to maintain the parish. Thus, chapels and small mission buildings, which are visited periodically by a priest, are not considered parishes. In most cases, all Catholics who live within the geographical area of a parish are considered the "designated people." In the United States, however, national and racial congregations have been established that often overlap territorial boundaries.[3] Sometimes members of racial parishes can decide

---

[1] Traditionally other institutions such as schools, hospitals and homes for the aged were segregated. The parishes were almost the only integrated units in the archdiocese.

[2] Canon 215, 1-3, quoted in Joseph H. Fichter, Dynamics of a City Church (Vol. I of Southern Parish, Chicago, 1951), p. 12.

[3] Ibid., pp. 12-13.

whether to attend the church set aside for them or the territorial parish. In South Louisiana Negroes are usually considered members of the racial parish; their connection with the territorial parish has been, and is now, rather vague.[1]

Parishes are not new to the Church, but in comparison to the mother institution they have a relatively recent history. They existed before the Council of Trent which convened in 1545, but only after that council was the parish structure of today organized. Many dioceses did not immediately heed the new regulations and as late as 1861 parish boundaries in New Orleans were rather haphazard.[2] Since the parish is an institution that is influenced by the society in which it exists, its functions will differ with changes in society. At all times, of course, the sacraments have been considered the essential function. Catholics are required to be baptized, married and confirmed in their parish, even though they may confess and attend Sunday Mass in other parishes or chapels. Nevertheless, it is possible for the parish to be viewed differently at different times. In one period it may be considered primarily as a mystical community attempting to achieve for its members through the liturgy a measure

---

[1] Rev. Stanley J. Iverson, Vice-Chancellor, Archdiocese of New Orleans, personal interview with author, New Orleans, 11 March 1965. Also Lanaux J. Rareshide, Assistant Chancellor, Archdiocese of New Orleans, letter 22 January 1971, to the author, writes that in one area of the city of New Orleans Negroes may "possibly" be members of both the territorial parish and the black parish at the same time.

[2] Circular letter of Jean Marie Odin, Archbishop of New Orleans, issued on 21 December 1861. Odin pointed out that the Council of Trent was strict about parishes and he believed that it was time for New Orleans to obey the council's directives. He therefore set up definite boundaries for all parishes in the city.

of the unity they share according to theological definition. At such times the spiritual aspects of the parish will be stressed in preference to its social functions. The parish can also be viewed as a multicentered social organization offering its members numerous avenues for personal expression that are at least partly oriented towards religious goals. When a parish is viewed in this way, emphasis is placed on the size of the parish plant and on the number of societies in the parish.[1]

Toward the end of the nineteenth century, Catholics in the United States entered a period of great consciousness of the parish as a social institution. Parochial schools were built and parish societies multiplied. A major portion of the social and educational life of many Catholics was connected to Church related functions and societies. Thus, many an active Catholic of 1900 would not have considered his life fully Catholic if he participated completely in the liturgy but did not seek any other involvement in parish life. It was in this milieu that the separate parishes were formed.

---

[1] J. Homeyer, "The Renewal of the Parish," The Parish, Hugo Rahner, ed. (Westminster, Maryland, 1958), pp. 127-128.

CHAPTER I

BLACK CATHOLICS AND THEIR CHURCH:
THE ANTE-BELLUM YEARS

    Structural differences only partially explain the Church's hesitancy to follow the Protestant lead to separate congregations. A fuller explanation requires a study of the relations of South Louisiana Negroes with their Church and to some extent with the state before 1865. It is for this reason that we first turn to a description of the unique position of black Catholics, both slave and free, in the ante-bellum Church.

    France and Spain controlled Louisiana until 1803. The close unity of Church and state in both of these countries was reflected in the slave codes which they enacted for Louisiana and which dealt with religious as well as civil matters. Bienville published the first Code Noir for the colony of Louisiana in March, 1724. The religious sections stipulated that all slaves were to be baptized into the Catholic Church, were to be instructed in religion, and were to observe Sundays and feast days like other Catholics.[1] The Spanish Black Code of 1789 provided for similar regulations and also stressed that Catholic slaves should be married by priests.[2]

    In the English colonies planters were not forced by law to provide religious instruction for their slaves, but slaveholders often did so voluntarily. Some missionaries who maintained that slaves were the spiritual equals of whites were resented by plantation owners. Many planters took some interest in the spiritual welfare of their

---

[1] William Renwick Riddell, "Le Code Noir," Journal of Negro History, X (July 1925), 325.

[2] Roger Baudier, The Catholic Church in Louisiana, p. 206.

slaves, however, and by the time of the American Revolution many slaves were members of a church.¹

Masters in French and Spanish Louisiana frequently had their slaves baptized in mass ceremonies on plantations, but further attention to their religious life was slight.² Slaves owned by Church officials were always permitted to practice their religion.³ Sometimes Church officials forced secular masters to obey the laws. For example, in 1738 the Superior Council of Louisiana was disturbed by charges of Father Mathias, Vicar General of Louisiana, that a high civil official had buried one of his slaves illegally. The Council ordered the body reburied in a cemetery with Church ceremonies. In theory at least, slaves were officially recognized as human beings.⁴

After the United States acquired Louisiana, Catholic masters continued to follow their former policies even though they were no longer required to do so by law. Most arranged for slave baptisms and attendance at church services was sometimes permitted. Old memoirs reveal that slaves occasionally received their first communion

---

¹Winthrop D. Jordan, White Over Black: American Attitudes toward the Negro, 1550-1812 (Chapel Hill, 1968), pp. 209-210, 418-419.

²Apparently most Catholics, white and black, received little religious attention after their baptism. In 1812 the entire state had twelve priests to care for thousands of Catholics. Baudier, Catholic Church in Louisiana, p. 266.

³Ibid., p. 115. Before 1729 the Jesuits had performed baptisms and marriages for their slaves.

⁴Charles B. Rousseve, The Negro in Louisiana (New Orleans, 1937), p. 39. Jordan in White Over Black, p. 210, suggests that in Catholic colonies the Church, being more authoritarian and powerful than the Anglican Church in the English colonies, could provide more protection for slaves.

at the same ceremonies as whites.[1] Church records contain permits indicating that some slaves were allowed to enter into Christian marriages,[2] and at least one New Orleans slave was married in the parlor of her master's home with white and black guests mingling at the ceremony.[3] Obviously, the majority of slaves who worked in the fields did not receive such thoughtful treatment. It is impossible to know how many slaves were married, as the old parishes did not always show race in marriage records,[4] but most likely the number was small. Although the religious passages were not adopted, slave laws of the State of Louisiana were influenced by the French and Spanish codes. The laws stated that masters had certain moral duties, and that slaves should be accorded just treatment. Moreover, in the Civil Code of the state, slaves were legally considered "persons."[5]

---

[1]Rousseve, *Negro in Louisiana*, p. 39. Rousseve quotes the unpublished memoirs of Pierre Landry who received his first communion with a mixed group in Donaldsonville sometime before 1850.

[2]A number of these old permits, signed by masters, and dating back to 1844 are on file in the New Orleans Archdiocesan Archives.

[3]Rousseve, *Negro in Louisiana*, pp. 174-175. Rousseve quotes Madame Frederic Allain, *Souvenires d'Amérique et de France, par une Creole* (Paris: Perisse Freres, 1882). She describes a slave wedding at her uncle's home in New Orleans and remarks that "tout le monde était heureux." This particular slave was considered one of the family.

[4]Reports of several old rural parishes in the New Orleans Archdiocesan Archives.

[5]Paul A. Kunkel, "Modifications in Louisiana Negro Legal Status under Louisiana Constitutions, 1812-1957," *Journal of Negro History*, XLIV (January 1959), 3-5.

In addition to the slaves, South Louisiana had a large free black population generally called "persons of color" or "gens de couleur."[1] Although the origins of this class are uncertain, it was in existence by 1722 and it increased in size in various ways. Some slaves were freed for "good and faithful service," a term often used when a man freed a concubine or blood relative. Black soldiers who performed bravely in battle were sometimes rewarded with freedom. Some slaves bought their own freedom or were purchased by relatives.[2] About 1800 refugees from the rebellion on Santo Domingo began seeking asylum in Louisiana so that, by 1809, several thousand of these exiles had arrived in the territory.[3] In 1830 free persons of color lived in almost every Louisiana (civil) parish. More resided in Orleans Parish than in all other parishes combined, but Pointe Coupee, St. Landry, St. Martin and Natchitoches parishes all had significant free black populations.[4]

As a class freemen of color achieved a measure of economic success and social prestige that contrasted

---

[1] Annie Stahl, "The Free Negro in Ante-bellum Louisiana," *Louisiana Historical Quarterly*, XXV (April 1942), 303, discusses the term "person of color." In Louisiana the term "Negro" implied slave status, while "person of Color" indicated a freeman. In 1810 a territorial court ruled that persons of color could be descended from Indians, free mulattos or a white parent and should be assumed to be free if there was no evidence to the contrary.

[2] Donald E. Everett, "Free Persons of Color in Colonial Louisiana," *Louisiana History*, VII (Winter 1966), 24,29,45.

[3] Alice Dunbar Nelson, "People of Color in Louisiana," *Journal of Negro History*, II (January 1917), 52.

[4] Carter G. Woodson, *Free Negro Heads of Families in the United States in 1830* (Washington, 1925), pp. 31-39.

sharply with the position of the slaves. Although most freemen worked as unskilled laborers, a remarkable number were skilled tradesmen, such as carpenters, masons, cigarmakers and shoemakers.[1] Black tradesmen were prominent enough by 1834 to form an organization, Les Artisans, which owned a private meeting hall.[2] A few freemen of color were professional men in the city, while others were planters who owned slaves.[3] Freemen of color paid school taxes in New Orleans but their children could not attend the public schools. Education was provided for some children in Europe but most children who attended school went to private Louisiana schools. Some Louisiana gens de couleur took an interest in literature and they produced a significant number of plays and a literary review. In 1845 they published Les Censelles, an anthology containing poems by seventeen New Orleans Negroes.[4] Freemen of color attained enough social prestige to be allowed to serve in colonial and American armies and militias.[5] A concert advertisement in 1807 illustrates their unique social position in New Orleans:

---

[1] Robert C. Reinders, "The Free Negro in the New Orleans Economy, 1850-1860," Louisiana History, VI (Summer, 1965), 274-275.

[2] Rousseve, Negro in Louisiana, p. 82.

[3] For examples of some of the large slave owners, see Woodson, Free Negro Heads, pp. 7-8. In 1830 Antoine Decuire of Pointe Coupee Parish owned 70 slaves, while Victoire Deslondes of St. John the Baptist Parish owned 52.

[4] Rousseve, Negro in Louisiana, p. 91.

[5] For a complete discussion of black soldiers in Louisiana, see Roland C. McConnell, Negro Troops of Ante-bellum Louisiana: A History of the Battalion of Free Men of Color (Baton Rouge, 1968).

> Free people of Color who may wish to attend,
> are informed that the Gallery usually appropri-
> ated for them is fitted up in the most convenient
> manner, and that no slave will be admitted.[1]

Legally, free people of color enjoyed most advantages of citizens, with the exception of political rights. Nevertheless, they were instructed never to "presume to conceive themselves equal to the whites."[2] As the conflict over slavery intensified, their status in society gradually declined. By 1842 free Negroes could no longer enter Louisiana from other states or nations. Further discriminatory laws passed during the 1850's prohibited them from incorporating any new religious, charitable, scientific or literary societies. Furthermore, they could no longer keep liquor stores or coffee houses. After 1857 no more slaves could be manumitted in Louisiana. Yet, the freemen of color retained some legal rights. They could still own slaves, buy and sell property, sue in courts, and possessed the right to trial by jury.[3]

Many gens de couleur, especially the leaders, left Louisiana in the late 1850's, but they were never legally expelled as they were from some other Southern states. At least once during this decade a newspaper publicly praised the free Negroes of New Orleans, calling them substantial property owners who were peaceful and orderly and possessed of a strong attachment to their city and state.[4] A pamphleteer, coming to their defense, wrote that freemen

---

[1] The Telegraph/Le Telegraphe (New Orleans), 13 October 1807.

[2] Kunkel, "Modifications," pp. 4-7.

[3] Robert C. Reinders, "The Decline of the New Orleans Free Negro in the Decade before the Civil War," Journal of Mississippi History, XXIV (April, 1962), 89-97.

[4] Daily Picayune (New Orleans), 9 January 1851, cited in McConnell, Negro Troops, p. 112.

of color in Louisiana were not like those elsewhere, and that, although the state was wise to forbid the entrance of freemen of color from other places, it should not expel its own people.[1]

Because of their status in society freemen of color occupied a position within the Church quite different from that of slaves. Two <u>gens de couleur</u> were married at St. Louis Church in New Orleans in 1724 in one of the earliest wedding ceremonies in the colony. According to reports of old New Orleans families, free people of color participated in the choir at St. Augustine's alongside whites. In some New Orleans parishes first communion classes were mixed at the altar rail regardless of race.[2] The occasional observation by ante-bellum visitors to New Orleans that masters and slaves knelt together in church is probably inaccurate. In all probability the Negroes referred to were free people of color.[3] In 1842 half the pews in the newly completed St. Augustine's church in New Orleans were rented by free Negroes. Slaves, on the other hand, sat in small pews on the side aisles which had been set aside for them. Other evidence of the freemen's established position is provided by the foundation of an order of black nuns. In 1842 a group of freewomen of color founded the Holy Family Sisters in New Orleans with the approval of the archbishop. The congregation devoted itself to teaching catechism to slaves and to caring for aged black women.[4]

---

[1] This information is in the pamphlet entitled, "The Free Colored Population of Louisiana," which was written by an unknown author shortly before the Civil War. It was printed by the Franco-American Printing Office in New Orleans and can be found in the New Orleans Archdiocesan Archives.

[2] Rousseve, <u>Negro in Louisiana</u>, pp. 40-41.

[3] Joe Gray Taylor, <u>Negro Slavery in Louisiana</u> (Baton Rouge, 1963), p. 138.

[4] Baudier, <u>Catholic Church in Louisiana</u>, pp. 365-397.

In the rural areas there were relatively few freemen of color and they usually did not occupy as high a position in society as their counterparts in New Orleans. Distinctions between freemen and slaves were not as pronounced as in the city; furthermore, rural whites were more afraid of slave uprisings. Thus, they tended to be suspicious of freemen of color who might help upset the status quo. One example of the lower status of freemen in the country is found in the act to incorporate the new church parish of St. John's in Lafayette Parish in 1824. The charter stated that the corporation was to be composed of "all the white Roman Catholics of the parish of Lafayette." Negroes could attend the church, but they were not permitted to become wardens.[1] Rural whites were also wary of religious instructions for blacks. It is further reported that some whites objected when blacks received communion at the same Mass.[2]

Slaves and free people of color retained their antebellum status in the Church during the Civil War. The only attempt that was made to grant them equal rights with whites quickly met with failure. While the war was still in progress the young pastor of a French parish in New Orleans, Father Claude Maistre, tried to change conditions within his jurisdiction and was promptly squelched. Father Maistre's congregation consisted of black and white parishioners and of the seventy-three children baptized at St. Rose de Lima in 1859, twenty-four were black. When the war came Father Maistre openly backed the Union to the chagrin of most of his fellow priests who supported the Confederacy. He was delighted with the Emancipation Proclamation and, inspired by that document, he noted in his parish register in December, 1862, that, "from the date

---

[1] <u>Acts Passed at the Second Session of the Sixth Legislature of the State of Louisiana</u> (New Orleans, 1924), p. 58.

[2] John T. Gillard, <u>Colored Catholics in the United States</u> (Baltimore, 1941), p. 69.

of January, 1863, acts for persons of color will be found inscribed in the grand register without discrimination, together with the whites." By doing this he flaunted archdiocesan regulations which called for separate registers for the two races.

Father Maistre also made public statements advocating elimination of discrimination. He succeeded only in angering the archbishop, Jean Marie Odin,[1] and provoking from others the accusation that he was inciting Negroes. Finally, on May 16, 1863, the archbishop imposed an interdict on Maistre's parish and suspended him from his duties as pastor. Odin then issued a pastoral letter, read in the city at all Sunday Masses, in which he warned Catholics to avoid St. Rose de Lima Parish as Father Maistre had been deprived of his spiritual faculties. Ignoring the suspension, the priest continued to officiate in his parish until he was eventually evicted. With the aid of some of his black and white parishioners he built a schismatic church, and only Archbishop Odin's successor, Napoleon Perche, archbishop from 1870 to 1883, persuaded Maistre to return to the Church. In 1870 the young priest wrote an open letter of submission and was officially reinstated. He remained in good grace with the official Church until his death in 1875.[2]

When the Civil War ended Church officials should have realized that the South was entering a new era, especially in relation to its black population. Nevertheless, officials in the Archdiocese of New Orleans strived to maintain Church life as it had been for one hundred and forty years. Their position was a rather paradoxical one. On the one hand they hoped to maintain the integrated parish and the semblance of unity among the races that this institution reflected, but on the other hand, they apparently were not prepared to tolerate a call for equality among the races in these parishes.

---

[1] Archbishop from 1861 to 1870.

[2] Roger Baudier wrote the typed manuscript history of St. Rose de Lima Parish in the 1940's. It is in the New Orleans Archdiocesan Archives with Odin's pastoral letter and a copy of the interdict.

CHAPTER II

FACTORS MAINTAINING INTEGRATION OF PARISHES
IN THE POSTWAR YEARS

For over twenty years following the Civil War blacks and Church officials alike preferred to allow matters in the parishes to remain as they had always been. The integrated status quo was not without its problems, but a number of factors operated to maintain it, and there were no attempts to begin separate parishes for Negroes.

In 1875 Canon Peter L. Benoit of the English Mill Hill Fathers came to the United States to investigate missionary possibilities.[1] He received a cold reception from Archbishop Perche, whom he visited on April 9, 1875. The archbishop was not interested in Benoit's offer of priests for New Orleans, for the prelate believed his diocesan priests provided adequately for black Catholics. He stressed that no missionaries were needed in the French areas of the city and, while he agreed that missionaries might find some work in non-French sections, he declined to make positive arrangements because of an impending trip to Europe.[2] Such vague encouragement did not lead to further developments, and the Mill Hill Fathers never came to New Orleans.

Canon Benoit was prepared for the archbishop's decision. He had already noticed that in the French sections "the position of the negro here and that of the clergy towards him differs materially from that of most cities." He also observed that "the negroes in the English portion of New Orleans are pretty much in the condition as they are in other cities." These Negroes, he

---

[1] The Mill Hill Fathers were the English predecessors of the American Josephite Fathers.

[2] Entry of 9 April 1875, Canon Peter L. Benoit Diary, Vol. 3, Mill Hill Fathers Archives (Copy in the Josephite Archives, Baltimore). Cited hereafter as Benoit Diary.

noted, were usually Methodist or Baptist.[1] Upon investigation he learned that most black Catholics lived in the French areas where they remained members of mixed churches. He also observed that clerical tolerance of Negroes was based in part on a very mundane consideration. Evidently the French priests were anxious to keep the financial support which blacks contributed to the parishes:

> The French clergy would not like to have them withdrawn from their churches because they are their chief support. The Creoles or real French are, I am sorry to say, as stingy here as in their own country. They support the theatres and go to them well dressed. But they don't support their churches in the same way nor are they frequenters of the Sacraments.[2]

Apparently the French priests continued to rely financially on their black parishioners. In July, 1884, the vicar general of the archdiocese informed Francis Xavier Leray, archbishop from 1883 to 1887, that most French priests would be disturbed if black members were removed from their parishes. Besides, the vicar general believed most blacks wanted to stay in the territorial parishes.[3]

Negroes who had been free people of color before the Civil War and who dominated black Catholic leadership were definitely not interested in separate parishes. They were proud of the position they traditionally held in the Church, and hoped to improve their status further. Naturally they resented any attempt to reduce them to the level of freedmen and they were shocked by the tendency

---

[1] Benoit Diary, 9 April 1875.

[2] Ibid. These French priests were usually natives of France as there were few American priests in Louisiana of French descent.

[3] Gilbert Raymond, vicar general, 8 July 1884, to Archbishop Francis Leray, New Orleans Archdiocesan Archives.

to compel all Negroes to sit in the pews which had been reserved for slaves. Nevertheless, they would not ask for separate parishes, preferring instead to demand better conditions within the regular parishes.[1]

Until 1888 archdiocesan officials held that separate parishes would not solve any problems for the Church. On June 19, 1888, the chancellor of the archdiocese, L. A. Chassé, set forth the official position of the Louisiana Church in a letter to the Commission for the Catholic Missions among the Colored People and the Indians:

> Distinct and separate churches are not advisable; experience has taught that the colored people prefer to come to mass and to the sacraments with their white brethren as it is done now in all the churches where French language is spoken.[2]

Chassé admitted that the Church was having problems with its black membership. He noted that many blacks were leaving the Church, but blamed black disaffection on the public schools. He argued that "what we need the most is the establishment of free colored schools to counterbalance the evil effects of the free public schools."[3]

The Catholic schools in the archdiocese were segregated by tradition, as were all other institutions except the churches. Until the 1880's most of them were run by religious orders as private finishing schools and academies. Every attempt to admit blacks to these schools had failed. When the Religious of the Sacred Heart and the Sisters of Mercy unwittingly admitted black girls to

---

[1] Rousseve, *Negro in Louisiana*, pp. 99-158.

[2] L. A. Chassé, 19 June 1888, to Secretary of the Commission for the Catholic Missions among the Colored People and the Indians, carbon copy in New Orleans Archdiocesan Archives.

[3] Ibid.

their schools, whites reacted angrily. The Religious of the Sacred Heart enrolled the daughter of a black state senator unaware that she was black. They immediately dismissed her when her identity was learned. Her father sued, but the court decided the case in favor of the nuns on the grounds that the girl had been registered under false pretenses. As a result of the court case, the school gained in both prestige and enrollment.[1]

The Sisters of Mercy came from Ireland to teach in the schools connected with parishes served by the Redemptorist Fathers. Mother Austin, the superior, was occasionally confronted by irritated whites who claimed that she had admitted black girls. If black descent was proven, she dismissed the child for fear that she might otherwise lose her white pupils. Since she had no support from the clergy, there was hardly any alternative. Nevertheless, Mother Austin, apparently a pluck woman, could resort to subterfuge on occasion. At least once she enrolled a black student without incident and simply told inquirers that the girl was only kitchen help. Such bravery received little praise; instead, "even priests had remonstrated with her for so dangerous an act."[2]

Although many of the religious orders hesitated to teach Negroes, even in separate schools, some parochial schools were organized for black children. When the Plenary Council of Baltimore in 1884 stressed the need for parochial schools attached to parishes, the Archdiocese of New Orleans attempted to carry out its directions. Parishes which could support schools began dual systems providing separate schools for blacks and whites. The black schools were often staffed by lay teachers instead of religious.[3]

---

[1] Baudier, Catholic Church in Louisiana, pp. 419-433.

[2] Benoit Diary, 7 April 1875.

[3] New Orleans Archdiocesan Book of Parish Statistics, 1888-1918, New Orleans Archdiocesan Archives.

The unique situation of integrated churches and segregated schools in Louisiana did not draw much comment from other parts of the American Church. Nationally, the Church adopted no specific program for black Catholics in the years immediately following the Civil War, and dioceses were free to devise their own programs. The Catholic Church had remained a united organization throughout the war without splitting into the sectional churches which characterized Protestant denominations.[1] Consequently, there was no proselytizing among Southern blacks by Northern Catholics in the hope of luring blacks away from a Southern Catholic Church. When missionaries did come during Reconstruction, they entered dioceses with the consent of the local bishops and were under their direction. Most bishops believed that officials in each diocese understood local conditions better than anyone else. Therefore, bishops were reluctant to offer unsolicited advice to one another.

The idea of local autonomy was reinforced with particular reference to race relations by the Second Plenary Council of Baltimore which convened in October, 1866. Forty-five bishops from all sections of the country gathered to discuss various problems affecting the Church in the United States. The Holy See had instructed them to give particular attention to the welfare of the newly freed Negroes, and one session of the Council was devoted to the Church's relations with its black members.[2] Since so few blacks in the United States were Catholic, the bishops viewed the problem mainly as one of conversion. They requested religious orders to begin work among Negro Americans and pointed out the great need for schools and orphanages. In particular, they urged priests from Europe to come to America to help convert blacks. The hierarchy specifically discussed the question of segregated parishes

---

[1] John Tracy Ellis, *American Catholicism* (Chicago, 1956), p. 91.

[2] Gillard, *Colored Catholics*, p. 113.

and decided that each bishop should be left to decide on their practicality, as conditions varied from place to place.[1]

In a pastoral letter issued to the clergy and laity at the close of the Council, the bishops urged all Catholics to cooperate with any plans that were devised for black Americans. It appears that some of them may have had second thoughts about the approach taken to the problem of slavery, for they expressed regret that the slaves had not been freed by "a more gradual system of emancipation." At the same time they hoped that they could help matters by extending to them "that Christian education and moral restraint which they so much stand in need of."[2]

Soon after the close of the Council large numbers of Catholic immigrants overwhelmed dioceses in the East and Midwest. Money and personnel that might have gone to Southern dioceses were needed at home. The Church in the large Northeastern and Midwestern urban areas was suddenly faced with problems of its own that made it difficult to give much attention to Southern blacks.[3] The bishops, meeting in 1884 at the Third Plenary Council of Baltimore, recognized that blacks were being neglected. To assure a regular, if small, flow of money to aid work with Southern Negroes and Western Indians, the Council decreed that every American parish should have an annual collection for Indian and Negro missions. The money was to be allocated to needy dioceses by a Commission for Catholic Missions among the Colored People and Indians, a board established by the bishops for that purpose.[4] Southern dioceses,

---

[1] Concilii Plenarii Baltimorensis II, Acta et Decreta, cap. IV, nos. 488, 489, 490, cited by Gillard, Colored Catholics, pp. 113-114.

[2] Ellis, American Catholicism, p. 172.

[3] Ibid., p. 101.

[4] Gillard, Colored Catholics, p. 116.

including New Orleans, began to send yearly reports to the Commission in the hope of receiving a share of the annual collection.

Obviously archdiocesan officials in New Orleans were pleased with the formation of the Commission and its promise of financial aid. Like most other Southern dioceses, the Archdiocese of New Orleans had not fully recovered from the Civil War and was deeply in debt. Archbishop Napoleon Perche had added to its financial burdens in the early 1870's with an ambitious program of expansion. Borrowing heavily from French and American creditors, he established a number of new parishes and schools. His efforts, however, were both financially ill-advised and ill-timed, for the economic panic of 1873 struck soon after the program began and the archdiocese was thrown into even greater debt and confusion. By the time of the archbishop's death, in 1883, the economic affairs of the archdiocese seemed hopelessly entangled--ninety per cent of Church property in the archdiocese being mortgaged. Perche's successor, Francis Leray, immediately realized that the archdiocese faced bankruptcy and he spent his entire episcopacy struggling to prevent complete financial collapse. Leray closed the diocesan seminary to save money and called a halt to further parish expansion. After considerable effort he compromised with his creditors, thus enabling his archdiocese to escape catastrophe. Only one parish, St. Joseph's in Baton Rouge, went bankrupt; the church building was sold at public auction in 1885.[1]

In addition to its shortage of funds before the 1890's, the archdiocese also suffered from a chronic shortage of priests. This lack of personnel impeded even normal parish expansion, to say nothing of its effect on the possibility of establishing black parishes. A native clergy was almost non-existant, and it was the general opinion of priests and laymen that Louisianians simply would not become priests.

---

[1]Baudier, Catholic Church in Louisiana, pp. 461-466. Also see the typed notes of Baudier in a file on the Church and Negroes, New Orleans Archdiocesan Archives.

Although there were a few early efforts to found seminaries, it was not until 1923 that a permanent major seminary was begun in the archdiocese.[1] Every archbishop was forced to recruit priests from Europe and other American dioceses, but enough priests could never be recruited and some of those who went to New Orleans proved to be unsuitable.

Within a few years, however, two developments occurred elsewhere in the country which eventually encouraged the establishment of separate parishes for Negroes in the Archdiocese of New Orleans. First, a congregation of priests, the Josephites, was founded in the United States to work exclusively with blacks. Then, a short time later, a wealthy heiress founded an order of nuns dedicated to working with Indians and Negroes and she pledged her entire fortune to the benefit of these two racial groups. Although neither of these new orders advocated segregation, the ironic fact was that only by establishing segregated church facilities could a diocese enjoy the benefits of their personnel and money. Their offer of services exclusively to black Catholics presented chancery officials with a temptation which they found hard to resist and was one factor, though certainly not the only one, that eventually led to the establishment of the separate parishes.

The religious predecessors of the Josephites came to the United States from England in 1871 to administer St. Francis Xavier parish in Baltimore, the first black American parish. The parish was established for the use of French-speaking descendants of refugees from Santo Domingo and had been dedicated on February 21, 1864.[2] The order planned to do missionary work "among the Pagans, especially the Negroes," their main goal being the conversion of black Americans.[3] At first the Josephites

---

[1]Baudier, <u>Catholic Church in Louisiana</u>, pp. 476-524.

[2]Gillard, <u>Colored Catholics</u>, p. 121.

[3]Peter E. Hogan, S. S. J., Josephite Archivist, Baltimore, letter, 31 March 1965, to the author.

were connected with the Mill Hill Fathers in England, but by 1893 they had completed arrangements to become an independent order with American headquarters. Over the years the order came to possess the resources and personnel needed to open new missions in Southern dioceses. The only way a diocese could induce the Josephites to come, however, was to open separate churches, as the priests would not work with whites.

The wealthy heiress who founded the order of nuns was Katharine Drexel, the daughter of a Philadelphia banker. She originally had planned to found a religious order of sisters dedicated exclusively to working among American Indians, but Pope Leo XIII persuaded her to include blacks in her apostolate. Her order, the Sisters of the Blessed Sacrament for Indians and Colored People, was organized in February, 1891.[1] Even before she had organized the religious community, Katharine Drexel sent money to Archbishop Francis Janssens of New Orleans for work among blacks. On three occasions between 1891 and 1895 Janssens visited her in Philadelphia.[2] Initially, the bulk of money she sent was used for schools, but eventually the Drexel fortune would also be used in establishing new black parishes.[3]

But Katharine Drexel and the Josephites had not been available during the immediate postwar years, and the parishes remained integrated because of the absence of strong

---

[1]Gillard, Colored Catholics, p. 125.

[2]Francis Janssens Diary, New Orleans Archdiocesan Archives. On December 30, 1889, the archbishop noted that he had received $300 from Miss Drexel. He saw here in Philadelphia in May, 1891, December, 1892, and September, 1895. He was also in continuous correspondence with her.

[3]A few of the early parishes built or renovated with Drexel money include St. Katherine's and Holy Ghost of New Orleans, St. Edward's of New Iberia and St. Paul's of Lafayette.

pressure for change. During Reconstruction there was no pressure from a Yankee Church in the North for change. In the eyes of many pastors the blacks were valuable members of the parish. While blacks were not satisfied with their reserved pews, there was little in the idea of racially separate parishes to attract the attention of black Catholic leaders who had hopes for a better situation within the context of the mixed parishes. White laymen looked upon blacks in a paternalistic manner and usually did not harass them. For their part, archdiocesan officials clearly preferred the mixed parish to any other arrangement. Even if they had not, the financial plight of the archdiocese in this period and its chronic shortage of priests would have probably proven an effective barrier to the establishment of new parishes designed exclusively for Negroes. Indeed, to French-speaking Catholics of both races, a radical departure from the status quo was more to be feared than sitting in the same church with people of a different race.

CHAPTER III

THE DECISION TO EXPERIMENT

The clergy and laity of South Louisiana did not suddenly decide that segregated parishes were advantageous to the Church. After 1888 a change in attitude and practice took place gradually which was only occasionally hurried along. But by 1918 the Church had developed a new policy regarding its black members. The period from 1888 to 1918 may be visualized as a transition period during which the Church was moving from a traditional arrangement of race relations to a radically new system which would ultimately usurp the sanction of custom and tradition. This period of transition may be divided into three phases. The first phase extends from 1888 to 1897 during which the first voluntary separate parishes were founded. The second phase extends from 1897 to 1909, a period roughly coinciding with the episcopacy of Archbishop Louis Placide Chapelle, and forms a sort of interregnum between the first and third periods. The third phase began in 1909 and came to a close in 1918. The first of these phases will be the subject of Chapters III and IV. The second phase is covered briefly at the beginning of Chapter V, but most of that chapter is devoted to the third phase.

Archbishop Francis Janssens was responsible for most developments during the first phase, which coincides with the years of his episcopacy. Janssens was actively concerned with the welfare of the Negroes within his jurisdiction and it was in the spirit of this concern that he formed the first voluntary separate parishes. He made this break with tradition, however, only because he believed that it would be beneficial to the Church. He was by no means certain that voluntary separate churches would solve any problems. His approach was characterized throughout by pragmatic experimentation.

The appointment of Francis Janssens to the Archdiocese of New Orleans was unexpected. New Orleans was not the kind of diocese that was thought of as a reward. With its large

debt and cantankerous populace, the archdiocese was a
challenge that many clerics preferred to avoid. But it
was popularly believed by clergy and laity, alike, that
the new archbishop would be French, as tradition required, and various French clergymen had been discussed
as likely candidates.

The Papal Bull appointing the new archbishop, issued in August, 1888, was not addressed to a Frenchman,
but to Francis Janssens, a Dutchman, who was Bishop of
Natchez. The new archbishop was no stranger to Southern
customs, as he had come to the Diocese of Richmond less
than a year after his European ordination and had served
there until his appointment to Natchez in 1881.[1] In New
Orleans he immediately attacked the archdiocesan debt by
an efficient arrangement of collections and bonds. To
win the confidence of the laity, he called a mass meeting
at a prominent New Orleans hotel on December 23, 1888,
at which time he outlined his fiscal program. The financially prudent laymen realized Janssens' competence
and responded by agreeing to contribute more money toward the liquidation of the diocesan debt.

Wasting no time, Janssens summoned an archdiocesan
synod to meet in May, 1889. He discussed the situation
of the archdiocese with his clergy, and together they up-
dated the diocesan regulations. Following the synod, diocesan priests were instructed to meet at conferences to be
held periodically throughout the extensive archdiocese.
The archbishop then turned his attention to the shortage
of priests. To him the idea of importing priests was
nonsense. He argued that he should not be expected to play
the role of an ecclesiastical beggar, scouring Europe for
priests. Louisianians could be priests. He scoffed at
old tales about local reluctance to take Holy Orders.
Build a diocesan seminary, he insisted, give intelligent
talks on the priesthood and the laity would encourage their
sons to become priests. Janssens got his seminary and
his theory proved right. When the new school was dedi-

---

[1]Baudier, *Catholic Church in Louisiana*, p. 467.

cated on September 3, 1891, the student body included a number of Louisiana boys.[1]

Janssens had awesome talents as an administrator, financial expert, and legal strategist. He was perceived as a threat by those who insisted that custom be preserved for custom's sake. To Francis Janssens the Church was an evolving institution whose members were more important than traditions. Certainly, he would have thundered against any suggestion to change Church doctrine, but many traditions had no connection with doctrine. Thus, Janssens was prepared to discard traditions if they caused undue difficulties for human beings. From the pages of his diary Janssens emerges as a man who could share, at least vicariously, in the experiences of the people of his archdiocese. Empathy, not paternalism, usually guided his actions.

Janssens was a man of rare common sense and human compassion. On his confirmation tours, he was quick to observe that rural priests lived a difficult life. On Sundays many of them said an early Mass in one town, and later, after a journey of several hours, they heard confessions and celebrated Mass again in another town. To the practical Janssens the communion fast was an unnecessary obstacle for the dedicated men. A drink of water on a hot day, a cup of coffee on a cold day, either would make a Sunday more bearable. On a trip to Rome, the archbishop asked if his priests might not drink water, tea, coffee, or milk before late Mass, but the Cardinal of the Sacred Propaganda replied that such privileges had never been and, therefore, could not now be granted.[2]

The archbishop also disagreed with the traditional views regarding marriages between Catholics and members of other religions. He did not promote such marriages but, if a couple of mixed religion decided to marry, he believed that they should be treated with dignity. In an

---

[1] Baudier, Catholic Church in Louisiana, pp. 475-477.

[2] Entry of June, 1894, Francis Janssens Diary, New Orleans Archdiocesan Archives. Cited hereafter as Janssens Diary.

unsigned article in The American Ecclesiastical Review of 1893, he wrote in favor of performing mixed marriages in church buildings. He also disapproved of the policy forbidding the banns for such marriages from being publicly announced.[1]

Janssens took a particular interest in the Italian immigrants in New Orleans and he persuaded Frances Xavier Cabrini, the Italian immigrant nun and first American citizen to be canonized, to send sisters to work among them. He even opened a chapel especially for Italians, but later he discontinued it as "the Italians did not seem to care for a special church."[2]

Being interested in the welfare of minority groups under his jurisdiction, the archbishop could not ignore the largest of these groups, the black Catholics. He wanted to know how many Catholics in the archdiocese were black, how they were treated in the churches, and whether the best means were being used to help them maintain the Faith. When his questions were answered with clichés and vague replies, he became determined to find out what life was really like for black Catholics.

The archbishop harbored enlightened attitudes about black Catholics. He regarded Negroes as fully developed human beings capable of the achievements of other men. He believed, for example, that young black men were perfectly capable of becoming priests.[3] In his writings there is little of the well-meaning, but condescending language, so often employed by nineteenth-century leaders when referring to Negroes. Further evidence of his ability to treat black Catholics as people can be found in an incident which occurred in 1891. During his confirmation tour of that year, the archbishop administered the sacra-

---

[1] Janssens Diary, 4 February 1894.

[2] Ibid., 17 April 1895. This chapel was a national church which the Italians were free to attend if they wished.

[3] Ibid., 1 September 1892.

ment in the chapel at Petite Prairie, a spot so remote that no archbishop had ever previously visited it. Because of the absence of hotels in the area, he was forced to spend the night with a family in the neighborhood and he chose to do so with a black family. It was a visit that he did not soon forget, for he remembered his host's address and six years later he sent it to the Josephites when they were preparing to go to Petite Prairie.[1]

Janssens' decision to experiment with separate voluntary parishes was based partly on his belief that Negroes were leaving the Church in alarming numbers and that separate parishes might slow down this trend. His belief that Negroes were leaving the Church was in turn based on an estimate of the black population in the archdiocese that was almost certainly excessive. In 1889 Janssens ordered all parishes in the archdiocese to take a census of black Catholics. The census was a failure because many priests did not cooperate with it. Of almost one hundred parishes, only eight replied in enough detail to be recorded. Moreover, some replies were meaningless. For example, the pastor of Immaculate Conception parish in New Orleans reported that he had thirty-one black parishioners, yet his baptismal records show that sixty-five black infants had been baptized in the parish in 1889.[2]

---

[1] The Colored Harvest, Vol. II, No. 7 (October, 1899). The Colored Harvest and St. Joseph's Advocate were two publications of the Josephites which contained a great amount of material on the works of the priests of that order. The reader may notice irregularities in the volume numbers of The Colored Harvest. It began publication in October, 1888, as a yearly, then in turn became a quarterly, a bi-monthly, a monthly and then a bi-monthly again. Some issues have no volume numbers, and at times one volume covered more than a year.

[2] New Orleans Archdiocesan Book of Parish Statistics, 1888-1918, New Orleans Archdiocesan Archives.

Despite the absence of an adequate census on which to base a population estimate, Janssens publicly announced that there were 75,000 Negro Catholics in the archdiocese in 1889. In a letter to a Father Greene, a Josephite in Baltimore, Janssens remarked that this number was "accurate."[1] The source of Janssens "accurate" figures remains a mystery. Probably he made estimates from old statistics which in turn had been gleaned from older estimates. The questionable accuracy of Janssens figures is further suggested by the greater caution of subsequent archbishops. In their yearly reports to the Commission for Catholic Missions among the Colored People and Indians, Janssens' successors sometimes put a question mark in the blank for black population. At other times they relied on Janssens' statistics and sent the same figures year after year.[2]

Janssens' announcement caused great anxiety and concern because officials generally believed that at least 100,000 Louisiana blacks had been Catholic by the end of the Civil War. Although a majority of the planters who moved into Louisiana after 1803 were Protestant Americans, churchmen later overlooked this fact and assumed that most slaveholders in South Louisiana had been Catholics, and that their slaves had been Catholics too. Even if large numbers of slaves had been baptized as Catholics, many probably were unaware of their baptism and could hardly be counted as Catholics in 1865. In view of these facts a more recent estimate gives the number of black Catholics in South Louisiana in 1865 as 50,000 rather

---

[1] Francis Janssens, 17 April 1889, letter to Father Greene, reprinted in St. Joseph's Advocate, Vol. VII, No. 3 (July, 1889), 638.

[2] Gillard, Colored Catholics, p. 97. Of course, this action could indicate unconcern, as well as caution.

than 100,000.[1] If this figure is accepted, black Catholics were a rather hardy group, for if the 75,000 figure for 1895 even approaches accuracy, fewer blacks were abandoning the Church than Janssens and his officials feared.

Another matter of concern to Janssens was that Negroes in the archdiocese did not have a chance to live in full parochial life. Although many parishes provided schools for black children, parishes generally did not allow blacks to assist officially in church ceremonies, to join that parish choir or other parish societies, or to sit where they wished in church. Janssens believed that the desire to participate in religious functions was driving many blacks to the Protestant churches.

Involvement in parish life was an essential feature of the complete Catholic life in the 1890's. W. Schwer, a European theologian, observed that the city parish was "not exclusively a religious association, but also a social grouping." He stressed the importance of involvement of urban people in the life of the Church. Those in authority should carefully draw Catholics "to the life of the parish through customs and usages adapted to their situation."[2]

---

[1] Quoted in Gillard, Colored Catholics, p. 94. The bishops were also confused about the total number of Catholics in the archdiocese and different statistics were sometimes issued for the same year. For example, in 1854 Archbishop Antoine Blanc, in a report to the Holy See, listed 95,000 Catholics for the archdiocese. The Catholic directory for that year listed 175,000 Catholics.

[2] Quoted in J. Homeyer, "Renewal of the Parish," p. 137. It is reasonable to believe that Janssens was interested in the theory as well as the practice of parish life. He was prudent but pragmatic constantly thinking about various schemes, trying

Janssens adhered to such beliefs and he felt compelled to find ways of giving devout Negro Catholics, who had no notion of apostacy, a chance to share in parish life.

Increasing racial tensions in society at large also affected the affairs of the Church and prevented black participation in parish life. During the 1890's there was a great rise in lawlessness and violence in Louisiana. Between 1882 and 1903 there were 285 known lynchings in the state and most of them occurred after 1890. The passage of Jim Crow laws in the 1890's also had its influence on the thoughts and emotions of Catholics. In 1890 the Louisiana legislature passed a law requiring separate railroad accomodations for blacks and whites. In 1894 an anti-miscegenation law was passed as well as a law requiring segregated waiting rooms at railroad depots. In 1898 a state Constitutional convention disfranchised blacks by imposing educational and property qualifications on the right to vote. The effectiveness of these measures is evidenced by the fact that 130,344 black voters were registered in Louisiana in 1897; by 1900 the number had dropped to 5,320. Louisiana in the 1870's and 1880's was no paradise for Negroes, but before the 1890's Negroes had more political and civil rights than at any time until the late 1950's.[1]

In this period race relations in church parishes also became more strained. Before 1900 the strained relations were more obvious in rural areas than in New Orleans. In his seventh annual report to the Commission for Catholic Missions among the Colored People and Indians, Archbishop Janssens noted that the

---

them out, reworking them, and trying them again.

[1]Dethloff and Jones, "Race Relations," pp. 301-323.

few white Catholics in the Petite Prairie district refused to attend Mass at the chapel there because the congregation was predominantly black. He added that "in some out of the way places where there is no church yet, and where the priest comes occasionally, there exists a great prejudice, and the white Catholics would wish to build churches and exclude the colored people."[1]

Janssens probably never learned of some incidents of racial unrest, but on his confirmation tours he could perceive that all was not well in the rural sections. The experience of one of the priests in the far western part of the archdiocese would not have surprised him. In his memoirs Father William Teurlings, pioneer pastor of South Louisiana, describes a troublesome first communion day in Creole in 1895. Creole, a small town in the marshlands of Southwest Louisiana, is located near the Gulf. At that time it was inhabited by rugged trappers and fishermen. A frontier spirit prevailed in the area, and racial hostility was sometimes expressed in a forceful manner. On the morning of the communion day, two men informed the priest that he should not allow Negro children to receive the sacrament at the same ceremony as white children. He was surprised and answered that he saw no reason to discontinue a practice that was common everywhere in Louisiana. Since they assured him that there would be trouble at this particular ceremony, he prepared himself and put his gun into his hip pocket. During the celebration Father Teurlings played the organ which was placed near the communion rail in full view of the entire congreation. The ceremony took place without incident, and the pastor was rather pleased until he found out why there had been no dis-

---

[1]Report of the Archdiocese of New Orleans to the Commission for Catholic Missions among the Colored People and Indians, reprinted in St. Joseph's Advocate, Vol. III, No. 10 (April, 1894), 530-540. Cited hereafter as Report to the Commission, 1894.

turbance:

> When I had sat down on my stool at the harmonium near the Communion rail my pistol had protruded through the cassock opening. When I put on my surplice, it had caught on top of the pistol. And there I sat, completely unaware that the miserable thing was sticking out all during the celebration . . . even while I played <u>Le Voici l'Agneau si Doux</u>... "Behold the Lamb so meek and mild."[1]

The more rugged and uneducated rural people were not alone in their dislike of associating with Negroes. The planters, too, were racially prejudiced. Monsignor F. L. Gassler described the attitudes of planters he knew:

> Of course we should not overlook the feeling of bitterness on the part of the whites against their former, now emancipated, slaves. This bitterness was intense at times. Like children bereft of their parents, those miserable ex-slaves were unable to provide for themselves. The impoverished plantation owners . . . paid their ex-slaves as small a pittance as they were obliged to do. It was barely enough to keep body and soul together. For the latter, the planter did not think himself obligated to provide.[2]

---

[1] William Teurlings, <u>One Mile an Hour</u> (New York, 1959), pp: 22-24.

[2] Msgr. F. L. Gassler, 31 August 1941, letter to Roger Baudier, New Orleans Archdiocesan Archives. Baudier had written to Msgr. Gassler, who was ordained in 1893, asking him to relate his impressions of the

Nor did all rural priests welcome their black parishioners. Some priests were overwhelmed with parishes that were much too large for one man to handle; others were simply prejudiced. Some, however, seem to have been genuinely concerned about the welfare of black Catholics. Monsignor Gassler noted that the priests in Lafayette and Opelousas "really cared for the colored Catholics," and that in St. Martinville the priests "had to rely on the colored Catholics as the main support of the Church."[1]

The discontent among white Catholics helps to explain why Janssens did not order the territorial churches to treat all members equally. Most likely he considered segregation and discrimination as social and political problems over which he had little control. If Janssens was not justified entirely in conforming to the context of his times, he cannot be condemned completely for not taking a more definite stand against racism. He lived in the 1890's, not the 1970's. Actually he was more forward-looking than the majority of his successors. He approved of black priests and did not regard Negroes as members of an inferior race. Still, he did not believe he could promise Negroes equal rights in parishes because of white hostility.[2]

The archbishop was confronted with a major dilemma. He thought that blacks were leaving the Church because they could not share in full parish life. But little could be done to help them when their mere presence in parish churches was causing increasing friction and insubordination among white Catholics.

---

status of black Catholics in the rural areas before separate churches were established. Cited hereafter as Gassler letter.

[1] Ibid.

[2] Report to the Commission, 1894.

Janssens found a solution in the concept of the national church. National churches for various ethnic groups were common in urban areas throughout the country. Such churches had had a long history in New Orleans. They were parishes of accomodation, organized to provide immigrants with familiar surroundings until they became accustomed to American ways. No member of any group was forced to be a member of a national church; if he desired, he could belong to his territorial church. Rather than helping immigrants, the national churches often emphasized the ethnic differences of their members and reinforced the prejudices of native Americans. Frequently, such churches helped preserve a ghetto existence for immigrants instead of helping them to enter the mainstream of American life.

The national church provided the model for Janssens' plans for black Catholics. For those who felt ill at ease and unwanted in the territorial parish churches, he would erect separate parishes in which blacks could participate fully without fear. White Catholics would be happy because Negroes who wanted to participate in parish life could now be referred to their own parish church. Those blacks for whom separate parishes held no appeal could remain as members of their old parishes. Janssens hoped that the national parish proposal would provide a workable solution for his dilemma. He had made no radical suggestions, as he advocated neither complete integration nor complete segregation. By stressing that the separate churches were experimental, he did not commit the Church to any concrete policy. If the parishes were successful, he could continue to build more of them as needed. Indeed, he probably thought that the plan could not possibly fail since he appears to have been convinced that black Catholics would flock to separate parishes.

He was certain that blacks were leaving the Church and he was just as certain that the attraction of an active parish life would serve as a strong reason for remaining in the Church and perhaps persuade some who had left to return.[1] He stressed the advantages of belonging to a separate parish such as being able to sit where one wanted, to join the choir and to enroll one's children as altar boys.[2] By allowing this participation the Catholic Church could compete with the black Baptist and Methodist churches in New Orleans.

Janssens considered separate parishes early in his episcopacy, but it was six years before he established the first one. Within a year after coming to New Orleans he was corresponding with Katharine Drexel and had received money from her for work with black Catholics.[3] By the 1890's he also received financial aid from the Commission for Catholic Missions.[4] As early as 1891 he sent a letter to France "to request the Marists to begin in this diocese parishes for the colored people,"[5] and by 1892 he had located an order, the Assumptionists, who were willing to come work with the black Catholics in Louisiana. Naturally he also discussed his ideas with his priests and fellow bishops.

In fact a fellow bishop may have planted the idea of the voluntary, national-type parishes for blacks in the archbishop's mind. In 1889 Janssens had written to Archbishop William Henry Elder of Cincinnati, a former Bishop of Natchez, asking advice about separate parishes. His old friend counseled against them, reminding Janssens that Negroes in New Orleans had always been opposed to separation. Elder's own opinion

---

[1]Report to the Commission, 1894.

[2]Times-Democrat (New Orleans), 20 May 1895.

[3]Entry of 30 December 1889, Janssens Diary.

[4]Entry of 15 November 1896, Janssens Diary. He had just received $3000 from this Commission.

[5]Entry of 30 April 1891, Janssens Diary.

was that the fewer distinctions and separations between the races the better. However, he offered a suggestion:

> How would it answer to put the matter practically to their own choice? - to begin with one separate Church for those who wish to go to it: to give the best accomodation you can for those who prefer to go with the whites.[1]

This is basically the approach that Janssens took.

Many priests of the Archdiocese of New Orleans were not enthusiastic about plans for separate churches. Janssens assured them that they would not lose white parishioners as the orders working with blacks would not have jurisdiction over whites. On his confirmation tours he emphasized that separate churches would benefit all by alleviating crowded conditions. In 1890 he noted that the church at Opelousas was too small, and he discussed the matter with the local priests, suggesting that it might be wise to build a church for the black Catholics.[2] Nevertheless, many priests remained skeptical. In 1894 Janssens admitted that "very few" of his priests favored the experiment of separate churches.[3] The attitude of the priests does not necessarily indicate great interest in the welfare of black Catholics. As noted earlier, some of them relied on the financial contributions of their black parishioners. Moreover, many French priests considered Janssens a Dutch intruder who did not understand the customs of South Louisiana

---

[1] William Henry Elder, 13 February 1889, letter to Francis Janssens, New Orleans Archdiocesan Archives.

[2] Entry written on a confirmation tour between 18 April and 13 June 1890, Janssens Diary.

[3] Report to the Commission, 1894.

as well as they did. They feared that some of his projects might damage the tranquility of the Church.[1]

Some black Catholics, too, opposed the plan. There is no evidence that any blacks requested the archbishop to begin separate churches. On the other hand, some blacks publicly condemned such parishes.[2] In 1894 Janssens complained about the attitude of New Orleans Negroes, some of whom were too vocal to suit him.[3] Some rural blacks, too, were hostile to the idea of separate parishes.[4]

Janssens faced many obstacles, but they did not stop him. He knew he might be disappointed in his hopes for the separate churches. He admitted that "a church for the colored people alone may deepen ill feeling and separate still more the two races, which now meet on common ground in the church."[5] Yet, only a trial would prove if this would be the case. A timid or excessively prudent archbishop would have hesitated to experiment. But Francis Janssens was neither timid nor excessively prudent.

---

[1] Baudier, Catholic Church in Louisiana, p. 477.

[2] This condemnation will be discussed in a later chapter.

[3] Report to the Commission, 1894.

[4] The Colored Harvest, October, 1889.

[5] Report to the Commission, 1894.

CHAPTER IV

JANSSENS' EXPERIMENT

Archbishop Janssens hoped to entrust a single religious order with the entire Negro apostolate, and he was pleased when, in 1892, the Assumptionists volunteered to assume responsibility for all work among black Catholics in the archdiocese. The Assumptionists were French missionaries with headquarters in Paris. The archbishop believed that their ability to speak French would be an advantage in the archdiocese, and the very fact that they were natives of France would make them more acceptable to the suspicious local French clergy.

Even the prospect of having French clergy working among the Negroes did little to allay the fears of the apprehensive New Orleans priests. At a lively 1892 meeting, several diocesan consultors warned Janssens that the Assumptionists would ask for jurisdiction over whites as well as over Negroes. After much discussion, four consultors agreed with Janssens' plans, while two dissented to the end. With characteristic diplomacy Janssens noted that "different opinions were expressed, but all thought it would be good to try it."[1] The next step was to arrange a meeting between Janssens and a representative of the Assumptionists. Father F. L. Renaudier, pastor of Paincourtville, went to Paris to discuss the work with the superior general of the Assumptionists. The superior accepted the general terms and sent one of his priests, Father Marcellin, to New Orleans to sign a contract with Archbishop Janssens.

In February, 1893 the archbishop and Father Marcellin met in New Orleans, and the Assumptionist approved the detailed contract with which he was presented. Father Marcellin's superiors in Paris refused to accept the

---

[1] Entry of 23 August 1892, Francis Janssens Diary.

contract because it limited their order exclusively, instead of primarily, to working with Negroes. In August the archbishop consented to allow the Assumptionists to hear confessions of white persons throughout the archdiocese, but he declined to give them further rights over whites.[1] Both sides found this an acceptable compromise, but the dire predictions of the New Orleans French clergy had already come true. Jurisdictional disputes had begun even before the missionaries arrived.

Nevertheless, the archbishop had faith in the Assumptionists and hoped that they would succeed in carrying out the plans specified in the contract. The contract deserves special attention as it was much more than a statement of formal terms. Written by Janssens himself, it was really a detailed outline of his 1893 plans for the entire black apostolate.[2] The contract began with the clear statement that the Assumptionists were to have complete jurisdiction over all work with black Catholics. The remainder of the document was divided into four main sections. Article Two discussed their work in the rural areas. Article Three explained how the Assumptionists were to obtain money for their work, and Article Four was a commentary on the importance of involving orders of nuns in work with Negroes.

---

[1] Father Marcellin's 1897 report to Archbishop Louis Placide Chapelle, entitled, "The Work of Color in Louisiana, its Origin and its History," New Orleans Archdiocesan Archives. Cited hereafter as Marcellin Report.

[2] Assumptionist Contract, New Orleans Archdiocesan Archives. Several copies of the agreement are in the Archives. All are handwritten in French, and the latest one was copied in 1897. The many later bitter arguments about the accuracy of the various copies of the contract arose over jurisdictional sections, not over the general outline. Cited hereafter as Assumptionist Contract.

Article One of the contract advised the Assumptionists in New Orleans to rent a hall situated in a black section of the city with a residence for the priests nearby. The hall was to be used as a chapel where the missionaries would celebrate Mass and conduct a variety of other ceremonies including baptisms, funerals and weddings. The priests could also hear confessions of both races in the hall. To prevent whites from taking over the new chapel, the contract specified that pews could be rented only to blacks. The contract stressed that black Catholics were not to be compelled to attend services at the chapel. They were to have full liberty to attend their regular parishes if they wished.

Once the chapel flourished, a school was to be established with sections for boys and girls. At night the school could be used for conferences, for meetings of the men and women's societies, and for any functions which the priests believed would attract Negroes. The contract expressed the hope that black Protestants, who were often reluctant to enter a Catholic church, might be attracted to such gatherings. Eventually several school halls were to be built throughout the city to serve as secondary parish centers. On feast days the societies from all these secondary centers could hold reunions at the central parish hall. By stressing school halls in the contract the archbishop was seeking to avoid criticism from blacks who were hostile to separate parishes. Article One concluded by emphasizing that the success of the experiment in New Orleans depended upon evening services, schools and home visits. Through these means, the priests would win the trust and affection of the Negroes.[1]

Article Two began by stressing that the center of all Assumptionist work was to be in New Orleans, and that the priests in the rural areas were to consider the city as their headquarters. The crux of this Article was addressed to the work to be done in rural areas. The plans for these areas were based on work already

---

[1] Ibid., Article One.

underway in the parish at Paincourtville, which will be discussed below. Upon their arrival in a district the Assumptionists were to contact prominent local blacks to determine the number of black Catholics in the area. At a propitious time the blacks were to be invited to a local home, where the priests would pray with them, teach them hymns, and give religious instructions. If the meetings were successful, the priests would take a collection in order to purchase a house or construct a hall. The building would be used for a school during the day and for church services in the evening.

The original contract allowed the Assumptionists no jurisdiction whatever over whites in rural areas. Their entire ministry was more limited than in the city. They were permitted to offer Mass at the halls, but baptisms, funerals and marriages were to take place in the territorial parish churches where parish priests would officiate. A few exceptions were made to this rule; the Assumptionists were permitted, for example, to baptize adult black converts and to regularize marriages that had already taken place.[1]

The priests would need, of course, an income to support themselves and to extend their work. Article Three indicated that the Commission for Missions could be relied upon for a sizable amount of money. Other sources of income would include charity bazaars, the sale of pews in the New Orleans black churches, and receipts of honorariums for marriages, baptisms, and funerals in New Orleans.[2]

Article Four discussed the importance of religious women to assist the priests. They could conduct schools, visit the sick, and instruct adults who had not made their first communion. Furthermore, the sisters could help manage the societies formed for the women and girls, and serve as figures of authority at assemblies which the priests could not attend. Special mention was made of the black sisters in New Orleans.[3]

---

[1] Assumptionist Contract, Article Two.

[2] Ibid., Article Three.

[3] Ibid., Article Four.

These were the terms of the contract to which the Assumptionists agreed, and with the difficulty over jurisdiction seemingly resolved, Father Marcellin returned from France to New Orleans to prepare for the arrival of his fellow missionaries, who were expected in October, 1894. Upon his return the archbishop informed Marcellin that the opening of the new parish in New Orleans was to be delayed indefinitely, and he suggested that the missionary might benefit by observing Father Renaudier's work at Paincourtville.[1] Father Marcellin was not alone in expressing surprise over this development. In 1893 Katharine Drexel had pledged $3000 for the new project, and in April, 1894, when the archbishop wrote to her concerning the donation, she replied that she had assumed from the long delay that the Assumptionists were not coming after all.[2] Fortunately she was still willing to send the money.

The French clergy were responsible, in part, for the delay. The archbishop had encountered sharp criticism from New Orleans priests when they heard that the Assumptionists were to be headquartered in the city. Janssens then decided that it would be imprudent to begin any parish in the city before 1895, and in June 1894 he visited Paris on his way to Rome and informed the Assumptionists that he needed more time for preparation.[3]

While negotiations in New Orleans concerning the new parish dragged on, the French missionaries, who by then had arrived in the city, were told by the Archbishop to go to the mission at Klotzville. Janssens' carefully organized plans were already going awry.

---

[1] Marcellin Report.

[2] Katharine Drexel, 9 May 1894, letter to Francis Janssens, New Orleans Archdiocesan Archives.

[3] Entry in May 1894, Janssens Diary, and also Marcellin Report.

Instead of being located at a headquarters in New Orleans as the contract provided, the Assumptionists were being shunted off to a rural area. By July 7, 1895, Father Marcellin had been given parish rights for the Klotzville chapel and the Assumptionists were at last installed in a mission, although not the one they had expected.[1]

Janssens was not banishing the Assumptionists to the forsaken wilds, however, for Klotzville was a promising country district in which the groundwork for mission activity among the blacks had already been laid by the French priests in Paincourtville. In the middle of the 1880's Father Jean Baptiste Lesaicherre had decided to give special attention to the black Catholics at Klotzville. Lesaicherre observed that many blacks in that small village about three miles from Paincourtivlle had left the Church, but those who remained were devout Catholics. During May they even held daily devotions in their homes and joined together regularly for the recitation of a communal rosary.[2]

Father Lesaicherre wanted to help these people to live a more complete Catholic life. Yet, he knew

---

[1] Entry of 27 July 1895, Janssens Diary. The extension of parish rights was a further deviation from the contract, which had not permitted the Assumptionists parish jurisdiction over rural Negroes. For 1896 and 1897 the Klotzville mission was listed as an actual parish in the Archdiocesan Parish Statistics Book, with a number of baptisms listed for each year.

[2] The Colored Harvest, October 1889. The Colored Harvest reprinted part of a letter written to the archbishop from a priest in Paincourtville. Unfortunately, the name was not included, but most likely the correspondent was M. A. Lesaicherre, brother of Jean Baptiste Lesaicherre. M. A. Lesaicherre was the assistant pastor at Paincourtville at the time.

that active participation in his church at Paincourtville was impossible due to the racial bias of many whites. His assistant eventually volunteered to go to Klotzville to preach at the services in private homes. Later the priests decided to build a small chapel there for blacks. At first the assistant met with some hostility from the black parishioners. He wrote to the archbishop:

> They seemed inclined to think our object was to prevent their going to church with the whites; and it was then I detected great symptoms of dissatisfaction, and likewise a movement to abandon me. Now, however, it is far otherwise, though prizing most highly their places in church, and following the exercises with the whites, they have a decided regard for their own little chapel, comformable to their especial taste in whatever flatters the eye and ear, and with its sermons and devotions particularly intended for themselves.[1]

When the blacks observed that the chapel was not a separate parish, they were less pessimistic. They organized their own society, "The Society for a Good Death," and held their own processions in honor of Mary and other saints. The priest showed lantern slides on biblical themes and became acquainted with the black members of his parish. The priests at Paincourtville, like Janssens, believed that blacks had to be provided with the opportunity to join in parochial life. In a letter to the archbishop Father Lesaicherre's assistant wrote, "You know better than I, Monseigneur, that they must have something themselves to do in the church; they must take part in the ceremonies."[2]

---

[1] Ibid.

[2] Ibid.

When the archbishop sent the Assumptionists to Klotzville, he hoped they would adjust to the new situation and make the tiny rural settlement the center of their apostolate. The Assumptionists worked faithfully at Klotzville, carrying on the work begun by the diocesan priests, but they did not forget the promised chapel in New Orleans and continued to remind Janssens about it. In spite of the contract Janssens did not choose to have the Assumptionists establish the first black parish in New Orleans. Any work the French missionaries began in the city would necessarily involve French-speaking Catholics, and the archbishop had had enough trouble already with New Orleans French-speaking Negroes and French priests to risk any more.

Janssens understood the hostility of the clergy better than the opposition of the blacks. He acknowledged that New Orleans blacks were unique but he failed to comprehend the various divisions within black society. He did not realize that the descendants of the freedmen of color did not like the idea of being classified with ex-slaves or their descendants. The former freemen of color were the largest group of black Catholics in New Orleans, yet Janssens frequently disregarded their wishes, not through malice but through ignorance. Janssens assumed that most descendants of freedmen were also Catholic. He did not realize that by 1860 the population of New Orleans was not entirely Catholic. Large numbers of slaves had attended Baptist and Methodist chapels provided by their masters and as freemen of color had belonged to the African Methodist Church, but the majority remained loyal to French cultural predispositions, including Catholicism. They accepted the privileges granted to them during the antebellum period in their church parishes as a matter of right.[1]

---

[1] Robert C. Reinders, "Church and the Negro in New Orleans, 1850-1890," Phylon, XXII (Fall, 1961), 245-246.

The former free people of color and their descendants looked upon the archbishop's plan for separate churches with resentment. They would have responded with more enthusiasm if he had built a Catholic high school for blacks. To this proud and conservative element of the population a separate parish meant encroachment upon old rights, while schools had been segregated by tradition. Furthermore, Catholic educational facilities were an immediate and vital need. Northern Protestants had founded black schools in New Orleans, including two universities, New Orleans and Straight, and Protestants were beginning to appropriate the prominent positions within the black community. Black Protestants sent their children to the universities and urged them into new business enterprises, such as insurance.[1] Black Catholics faced a dilemma. Their children could obtain an education only at the segregated public high schools, the state university for blacks, Southern, or the Protestant universities. They believed that the young people might face a constant barrage of anti-Catholic indoctrination in such institutions. Their only alternative was to allow black Protestants to dominate the business field. Janssens was uneasy when he saw Catholics attending Protestant and public schools, where he assumed the students heard much against the Church. Since the educated people were respected, he believed that they exercised "by their better secular education an influence over their race to the detriment of the Church."[2] Nevertheless, by establishing a separate parish for blacks, he adopted a course that could only further estrange the educated descendants of the freemen of color.

---

[1] August Meier, *Negro Thought in America, 1880-1915: Racial Ideologies in the Age of Booker T. Washington* (Ann Arbor, 1963), p. 152.

[2] Report of Archbishop Francis Janssens to the Commission for Catholic Missions among the Colored People and Indians, reprinted in *St. Joseph's Advocate*

Janssens did not have much choice. He wanted a school and a church and for both he needed money, a building, and personnel. In 1895 all three were available for a non-French church, so he acted quickly. In that year the Vincentian Fathers of St. Joseph's parish built a massive new church several blocks down Tulane Avenue from their old one. They hoped to help liquidate the debt on the new building by razing the old church and selling the property. Janssens, however, asked them to reconsider their plans. The abandoned church was small and in bad repair. Nevertheless, it had many advantages. It was centrally located, convenient to black neighborhoods, and distant from French parishes. If the Vincentian Fathers would agree to provide priests for the church, Janssens could obtain funds for restoration. The Vincentians gave their consent, and Katharine Drexel gave $5000 for the renovation.[1]

At last the archbishop saw his scheme taking concrete shape. Soon after the decision was made, work was begun to transform the old St. Joseph's, a territorial church, into a black national church to be called St. Katherine's in honor of Katharine Drexel and her patron saint.[2] Father F. V. Nugent, C. M., supervised the extensive repairs. A reporter for the Times-Democrat commented enthusiastically on the new appearance of the church:

III (April, 1894), cited hereafter as Report to the Commission, 1894.

[1] St. Katherine's Parish Record, New Orleans Archdiocesan Archives. Cited hereafter as St. Katherine Records.

[2] Note that although the parish was named in honor of Katharine Drexel, the spelling of the name was not the same.

>One unacquainted with the fact that it is an old church built over would never recognize the fact from an observation of either its interior or exterior. The general appearance of the church on the outside is very pretty, while the fresco and design work in the interior is especially beautiful, and the work around the altar elaborate in conception and finish.[1]

Nevertheless, the building lacked some frills that nineteenth-century Catholics enjoyed in their churches. A newsman from the Daily Picayune observed that the sacred edifice was "elegant and comfortable" but remarked that the walls were "bare of any sacred paintings, pictures or statuary."[2]

Eager to make a success of the church, the priests of St. Katherine's organized parish societies even before the formal dedication. At least some black New Orleanians cooperated as a number of women organized a Sanctuary Society, while a group of men formed a reception committee to plan the dedication ceremonies. Young boys became acolytes and learned the duties of altar boys. Mrs. Mamie Power Aitken, the organist, directed the new choir which was to be a major attraction at St. Katherine's. As was customary in New Orleans, the choir included instrumentalists, such as violinists, as well as the vocal section.[3] The black

---

[1] Times-Democrat (New Orleans), 20 May 1895, p. 3.

[2] Daily Picayune (New Orleans), 20 May 1895, p. 10.

[3] Times-Democrat, 20 May 1895, p. 3. The reader must not draw false conclusions. The inclusion of musical instruments in the choir does not indicate that Negroes wanted more lively music than was available in territorial churches. Unlike many Protestant denominations, music in a black Catholic church was almost identical to music in a territorial church.

school attached to St. Joseph's became part of the St. Katherine complex with lay white women teaching the classes.[1]

Some blacks censored Archbishop Janssens when work was begun on St. Katherine's. In 1894 the archbishop had admitted that a number of blacks with French cultural backgrounds did not want a separate church. He had noted that they thought he wanted to "separate the races and widen the gap which exists between the white and colored population."[2] By 1895 he had not allayed their fears:

> In the city we are hampered by a small portion of the colored people, most of them light mulattoes, and politicians, who abuse me in public print for attempting to begin a new church for the colored people. These persons aim at a greater equality with the whites, politically and socially, and also in the churches, and they pretend that I wish to accentuate still more the separation between the churches.[3]

While they may not have abused the archbishop, leading blacks certainly criticized him for his decision. Prominent descendants of free people of color had organized the Comité des Citoyens, a committee designed to challenge Jim Crow laws, and as such they informed Janssens that instead of helping Negroes he was placing the stamp of ecclesiastical approval on

---

[1] St. Katherine Records.

[2] Report to the Commission, 1894.

[3] Report to the Commission for Catholic Missions among the Colored People and Indians, 1895, quoted in Gillard, Colored Catholics, p. 122.

unchristian discrimination.[1] Before the dedication of St. Katherine's the committee urged black Catholics to have nothing to do with what it called "the Jim Crow church." A resolution was published in its newspaper, The Daily Crusader:

> Resolved, that the Citizens' Committee most earnestly protest against the newly reparied St. Joseph Church as a separate place of worship for any class of the faithful and most anxiously hope that the colored Catholics will better show their disapproval of the same by abstaining from the dedication services and from any subsequent frequenting of said church. . . .[2]

Nevertheless, large crowds were present at the dedication on May 19, 1895.[3] The archbishop devoted the major portion of his sermon that day to a justification of the establishment of a separate church for black Catholics. Noting his firm belief that all men were equal before God, he emphasized that the separate church did not rest upon notions of black inferiority. The church was established, Janssens insisted, because of "the peculiar conditions" that existed in the South and the virtual impossibility "for white and black to mingle together and freely assist at religious services

---

[1] Rousseve, Negro in Louisiana, p. 139.

[2] The Daily Crusader (New Orleans), 14 February 1895, quoted in Rousseve, Negro in Louisiana, p. 158.

[3] Entry for 19 May 1895, Janssens Diary. The archbishop wrote that "the Church was packed with colored people who seemed much interested." Of course, his definition of "packed" might have been different than that of black leaders, who might have estimated that the numbers were smaller.

in the same edifice."[1] Since the Archdiocese of New Orleans had a large black Catholic population, he had given and would continue to give special attention to their needs. The creation of St. Katherine's was an example of that special attention. He hoped that black Catholics would use St. Katherine's, but hastened to add that blacks would not be forced to attend this church. It was to be a church of accomodation, not coercion:

> Here in this church the colored people will be at home. . . . It is for all the colored people of New Orleans but none of them are compelled to come here. If they prefer to remain in their own parish they are at liberty to do so, but I want to say that St. Katherine's church is for them at all times, if they want their children to make their first communion or if they desire to attend mass or services or go to confession or get married, and have their children baptized here.[2]

To lessen the fears of the French priests, Janssens specifically limited the jurisdiction of the new parish. The priests in charge could not administer the sacraments to whites, except to hear confessions and to give communion. No pews could be rented to whites.[3] The priests were further pacified by the fact that the archbishop had chosen the Vincentians to staff St. Katherine's. That order already had a territorial parish of its own in New Orleans and it was expected that the Vincentians at St. Katherine's would be respectful of jurisdictional boundaries.

---

[1] The Daily Picayune (New Orleans), 20 May 1895, p. 10.

[2] Ibid.

[3] Entry of 19 May 1895, Janssens Diary.

School and baptism records suggest that most blacks remained members of the territorial parishes. Nevertheless, enough blacks attended the new church to justify its existence in the mind of the archbishop. Many found the parish more attractive when Father Peter Cuddy, C.M., introduced various recreational activities. He realized that most places of entertainment in the city were closed to blacks, and after 1902 he formed a parish committee, the "Old Willing Workers," who were in charge of entertainment. All New Orleans blacks were invited to St. Katherine's for plays, dances and music festivals.[1]

As early as 1897 Archbishop Janssens decided to organize another black parish in New Orleans, and this time he called on the Assumptionists for help. In February, 1897 Janssens asked Father Barnabe of the Assumptionists to look for a house with sufficient land for expansion. He decided to divide the city into two sections. The Vincentians would care for blacks in the English-speaking areas, while the Assumptionists would work in the French sections of the city. Father Barnabe located suitable property on Esplanade Avenue, and the archbishop indicated that he would contribute to the purchase price.[2]

But the archbishop died in June of 1897 before the Assumptionists could move into their new quarters on Esplanade Avenue. Monsignor J. B. Bogaerts, who was appointed Archdiocesan Administrator, wisely decided to delay the opening of the chapel until a new archbishop was appointed. In September Bogaerts received an angry petition from the pastors of five parishes located near the Assumptionist property. The irritated priests demanded a re-examination of the Assumptionist contract.[3]

---

[1] St. Katherine Records.

[2] Marcellin Report.

[3] It seems incredible that anyone could still be serious about the Assumptionist contract which had been ignored and violated for four years. However, it was a source of great agitation for the French priests.

Their fears were based on the belief that the Assumptionists would attract white parishioners away from their parishes. They realized that Janssens had promised the Assumptionists a black parish and they unenthusiastically admitted that such a parish might succeed. If their black parishioners wanted to attend it, they were willing to sacrifice the monetary contributions the blacks made to their churches. They did not intend, however, to sacrifice their white parishioners also.[1]

Archbishop Louis Placide Chapelle, who was installed as archbishop in 1898, agreed to study the contract, and the Assumptionists were informed of the delay.[2] It was a delay that became permanent. The Assumptionists were never to open the chapel on Esplanade Avenue. They experienced similar problems in the parish at Klotzville. The pastor at Paincourtville complained that the extension of parish rights to the order at Klotzville simply established a parish within a parish. He resented the intrusion upon his "rights."[3] By 1899 the Assumptionists could no longer support the church at Klotzville and when the chancery sent no financial aid, they withdrew permanently from the archdiocese.

The withdrawal did not end the efforts to establish rural black parishes. Because of the early hostility toward the Assumptionists Janssens had been in contact

---

[1] Pastors of St. Rose de Lima, Notre Dame du Sacre Coeur, St. Boniface, St. Augustine and St. Ann, 18 September 1897, letter to J. B. Bogaerts, New Orleans Archdiocesan Archives.

[2] Entry of 11 February 1898, Janssens Diary. For a short period Bogaerts and Chapelle continued to write in the diary. Chapelle made the above entry.

[3] J. N. Massardier, 12 July 1895, letter to Francis Janssens, New Orleans Archdiocesan Archives.

with various religious orders long before his death.
No order attracted more of his attention than the
Society of St. Joseph, or the Josephites, a young
American order. He had encouraged young men from the
archdiocese to join the order and in 1892 two young
Negroes from New Orleans entered the Josephite seminary.[1] In subsequent years other young blacks from
Louisiana began to study with this order. By 1895
at least one white Louisianian had been ordained a
Josephite. The archbishop hoped that these men would
someday return to their home state to help alleviate
the shortage of priests.

Due to the growth of the Josephite order, the
superior, J. R. Slattery, assured the archbishop that
"after September 1897, we shall be prepared, if you
want us, to take up the Colored work in your Diocese."[2]
There would be no jurisdictional problems, Slattery
wrote, as the Josephites "have nothing to do with the
whites in our own Churches, not even hearing their
confessions."[3] A formal agreement was signed on
February 1, 1897, in New Orleans by Janssens and Slattery. The Josephites agreed to "take charge of the
spiritual and temporal interests of the Colored people of Palmetto," a small town approximately fifty
miles west of Baton Rouge. They further promised
"not to interfere in one way or another with the Catholics of any congregation except they be Colored."
The archbishop agreed not to allow other priests to
work with the blacks in the Palmetto area "as long
as the Fathers of St. Joseph's Society shall be faith-

---

[1] Entry of 1 September 1892, Janssens Diary.

[2] J. R. Slattery, 2 November 1896, letter to
Francis Janssens, New Orleans Archdiocesan Archives.

[3] J. R. Slattery, 12 November 1896, letter to
Francis Janssens, New Orleans Archdiocesan Archives.

ful to their duty and be able to provide for the spiritual wants of the Colored people."[1]

Before Archbishop Janssens died in June, 1897, he had written explicit directions for the Josephites, and consequently they were allowed to begin their work before the appointment of a new archbishop. Young Father Pierre O. LeBeau, S.S.J., was appointed the first pastor of the new parish in the Palmetto area. After conferring with the administrator in New Orleans, he went to Washington, Louisiana, to collect the parish records. An elderly priest at Washington, aware of the many hardships of a rural pastor, remarked to Father LeBeau, "You will be miserable, but I hope it all works out for the best." Undaunted, the priest set out for Petite Prairie, going first to Palmetto by train, and then by buggy to the settlement, which he reached on August 30, 1897.[2]

Petite Prairie was a rural settlement eight miles from Palmetto, the site of the nearest post office and railroad depot. After 1874 a former general store had served as a chapel for the people of the vicinity, most of whom were black. Once a month, on a weekday, a priest from the mother parish in Washington, Louisiana, about twenty miles distant, came to say Mass. The neighboring parish in the opposite direction was at Port Barre, also twenty miles away. The records of the Petite Prairie mission had been kept at Washington, and the people had had to go there for certain sacraments.

Archbishop Janssens had become very interested in Petite Prairie after a confirmation stop in 1891. He

---

[1] Josephite Contract, New Orleans Archdiocesan Archives. Palmetto in the contract refers to the chapel eight miles away at Petite Prairie. There was no real village at Petite Prairie in 1897. It later became the town of LeBeau, named for Father LeBeau.

[2] Pierre LeBeau, 7 September 1897, letter to J. R. Slattery, reprinted in The Colored Harvest, I (January, 1898), 248-249. Cited hereafter as LeBeau Report, 1897.

gave serious thought to the area's need for a resident priest.¹ The Josephites were the ideal priests to invite, as local circumstances fitted in with the aims of the order. Although most of the blacks at Petite Prairie were Catholic, Baptists were also numerous, and they would provide the priests with a source of converts. The surrounding area was genuinely mission territory, populated by poor people who had little, if any, religious training.

The new Immaculate Conception parish was detached from the parish at Washington. Naturally, the few black Catholics in Washington continued to attend the parish church there. Immaculate Conception, itself, turned out to be an integrated parish, in reality, if not officially. Although the Josephites had agreed to minister only to blacks, many whites, probably attracted by LeBeau's personality, attended Mass at Immaculate Conception and brought their babies to be baptized there.² Apparently the pastors at Washington and Port Barre did not mind this invasion of their jurisdiction, as they did not complain about it. Most likely they were pleased that their more remote parishioners could receive the regular attentions of a priest.

Few parishes in South Louisiana were fortunate enough to have as pastor a native who could speak the French dialect of the area and who had grown up with its customs. Father LeBeau, the son of a Pointe Coupée planter,³ was familiar with the food, language, living conditions and farming methods in Petite Prairie. No one could call him an outsider, and he could perform his work with assurance and confidence, as he was a member of a prominent local family.

---

¹The Colored Harvest, II (October 1899), 119.

²New Orleans Archdiocesan Book of Parish Statistics, 1888-1918, New Orleans Archdiocesan Archives.

³Father LeBeau's home parish of Pointe Coupée was a few miles from Petite Prairie.

The young priest was quite busy during his first week at Petite Prairie. Because the Texas and Pacific Railroad was only nine acres from his mission, he was able to arrange with the company to put a flag station within walking distance of the church. With a train stop so close, he planned to request a post office for the settlement. LeBeau informed his superior that he hoped to attract a new storekeeper to Petite Prairie because he believed the local merchants swindled black customers. During that first week he stayed with a black family who allowed him free room and board and the use of a horse and buggy. He needed his own house, however, and before the week was out a parishioner had donated seven acres of land for a church and residence.[1] The next week the whole community hauled lumber from the depot and began constructing the residence. Father LeBeau noted that even some Baptists helped to build his house.[2]

For three years the parish continued to use the old chapel which had been built many years before. Then in 1900 the dilapidated building was replaced with a new structure. The congregation raised the money and volunteered their labor. A local white Protestant sold LeBeau cypress at cost price, and again the whole community hauled wood. The Methodist minister, a former Catholic, cut the shingles, charging only half the usual rate.[3] Father LeBeau's optimism and positive attitude toward his parishioners greatly aided Immaculate Conception to become a thriving parish in a short time. He regarded his parishioners as individuals and appreciated the fact that they shared with him a unique culture:

---

[1] LeBeau Report, 1897.

[2] Pierre LeBeau, letter (no date), to J. R. Slattery, reprinted in The Colored Harvest, II (October, 1898), 50-51.

[3] The Colored Harvest, II, No. 11 (October, 1900), 204.

> The people are thoroughly French and Southerners in manner, affable, gentle, docile, polite in the extreme. . . . You would never imagine you were speaking with colored people as in the North and Protestant South if it were not for their skin.[1]

As a result of Father LeBeau's success at Petite Prairie, the Josephites were often invited to become pastors of other black parishes.

Janssens, of course, never had a chance to evaluate his various experiments. When he died separate parishes had not been established long enough for him to be certain that they should be continued. Yet, he had had two years to observe and evaluate St. Katherine's and, based on that experience, he concluded that a second church was needed in New Orleans. He had also established the parish at Petite Prairie. Hence, Janssens seems to have made a tentative decision that the separate parishes were useful. It is true that he did not observe the Josephites, but there seems every reason to believe that he would have been completely satisfied with the Petite Prairie parish. Only total indifference and non-support by black Catholics could have stopped the experiment by 1900. Although there was definite black opposition to separate parishes, the fact that some black Catholics attended services in places set aside for them made the experiment seem worth continuing in later years.

---

[1] LeBeau Report, 1897.

CHAPTER V

THE EXPERIMENT BECOMES PERMANENT

Louis Placide Chapelle was named Archbishop of New Orleans in 1897 and was installed in February, 1898. He had been considered previously for the position, but instead had been made Bishop of Santa Fe. Chapelle, a native of France, had come to the United States as a young seminarian. After his ordination, he had served in Washington, D. C., where he had become the friend of many politicians and foreign diplomats. A close student of international affairs, he was the pope's logical choice as Apostolic Delegate to Puerto Rico, Cuba and the Philippines during the troubled times of 1898.[1] Owing to the responsibilities of this position, he spent little time in his own archdiocese. As a result, many Church projects were temporarily suspended, among them the creation of new black parishes.

Thus, there was a lull in the transition to segregated parishes, which lasted until 1909, when Chapelle's successor, James Hubert Blenk, S. M., resumed the work begun by Janssens. It was during Blenk's tenure as Archbishop of New Orleans that systematic segregation was given official sanction and became the established practice within the Catholic Church of South Louisiana.

Blenk, like Janssens, was an organizer and administrator. He was born in Bavaria and raised in New Orleans. Before being named Bishop of Puerto Rico in 1899, he had been a pastor in New Orleans and president of Jefferson College in St. James (civil) Parish.[2] The

---

[1] Baudier, *Catholic Church in Louisiana*, pp. 493-495.

[2] Ibid., p. 507.

new archbishop was well known and respected in New Orleans and the surrounding area. His previous work in the archdiocese exempted him from accusations of being an outside meddler, and he could proceed with a variety of projects knowing that he was supported by most priests in the archdiocese.

At first Blenk approached the matter of separate parishes gingerly, establishing only three during his first eight years as archbishop. However, by 1915 he had become convinced that more separate parishes were necessary. In that year he divided the entire city of New Orleans into sections and within five years six new black parishes were founded in the city.[1] In addition to the city parishes, he established several new segregated rural and small town parishes. This sudden spurt of activity might seem a startling development in the usually cautious Archdiocese of New Orleans. However, the status of Negroes had been deteriorating since the 1890's, and by 1915 white Catholics were much less tolerant than when Janssens was archbishop.

The decline in Negro status in the Church was national as well as local. A few years earlier members of the hierarchy like Archbishop Janssens and James Cardinal Gibbons of Baltimore had been strong backers of black priests. By 1915 feelings had hardened against black clergymen, and the Josephites were advised by Church officials not to preach to blacks about vocations. A Josephite official, John Albert, complained to the Apostolic Delegate, noting that many restrictions were being placed on his order. In one six month period the Josephites had had twenty-four applicants for admission. They had been forced to deny entrance to the fourteen Negroes among them.[2]

---

[1] The Colored Harvest, Vol. XXIX (February-March 1942), 4.

[2] Albert Sidney Foley, S.J., God's Men of Color: The Colored Catholic Priests of the United States, 1854-1954 (New York, 1955), p. 92.

Prior to 1907, three blacks had become Josephite priests, but no more were ordained until 1941, although a few were admitted to the seminary during the intervening years.[1] The subsequent dearth of black priests gave rise to a myth that blacks did not want to become priests, and that as a race they had not progressed far enough to put forth likely candidates for ordination. The candidates were available, but white prejudice, both clerical and lay, kept them out of the seminaries. Janssens had scoffed at the idea that Louisiana men would not become priests, but for many years other bishops were too timid to ignore the racial myth. Even Cardinal Gibbons, who had been a staunch

---

[1] Father Peter E. Hogan, S.S.J., Josephite Archivist, letters, 31 March 1965 and 30 April 1965, to the author. Father Hogan believes that the subject of Negro priests "deserves a definitive, well researched and balanced study." Such a study would have to investigate both theory and practice regarding Negro priests. No bishop ever spoke against Negro priests in theory, but their actions spoke otherwise. Father Hogan suggests that Father John R. Slattery, the first Superior General of the American Josephites, had a definite influence on the changing attitudes. Father Slattery supported Negro priests, and at the first Mass of a Negro, John Henry Dorsey, in 1902, Slattery "attacked the Irish clergy for their treatment of Negroes." Later a controversy developed when Monsignor Starr of Baltimore defended the Irish clergy. The local newspapers gave wide coverage to the disagreement between Slattery and Starr. Eventually, Slattery left the Catholic Church, prodded only in part by his difficulties with Irish priests. He was also an adherent of the Modernism heresy, which was his main reason for leaving the Church. Nevertheless, as Father Hogan points out, "If the strongest and most vocal proponent of the Negro Catholic clergy takes such a tumble, the cause with which he is associated, in the eye of the public is also bound to come under suspicion."

advocate of black priests, withdrew his support of black clerics. His advisors persuaded him that his favorable attitude was unwise and after 1907 he did not preside at any more black ordinations.[1]

Gibbons' eulogy at the 1913 funeral of a Louisiana black priest, John Plantevigne, is representative of the American hierarchy's attitude towards Negroes at that date:

> Who was the greater: John the Baptist or Herod? John the Baptist was cast into prison and was there beheaded, while Herod enjoyed all the freedom and happiness that civil liberty can afford; yet John the Baptist was the greater because he was free from the slavery of sin, and therefore enjoyed the testimony of a good conscience. The Apostles were calumniated and thrown into prison...
> They did not enjoy civil liberty, but their hearts were clean and stainless... You should prove yourselves worthy of the love and respect of your fellow-citizens, and if you do, civil rights will never be denied to you...[2]

This was the same Gibbons who had shared Janssens' hopes for Negro Catholics. Many bishops, including Archbishop Blenk, tended to follow the lead of Cardinal Gibbons.

Blenk did not want black pastors in his archdiocese. He did not even like the idea of allowing some black priests to enter the archdiocese on temporary church business. In 1909 he forbade entrance to one of Louisiana's native priests, John Plantevigne. The arch-

---

[1] Foley, God's Men, p. 93.

[2] James Cardinal Gibbons eulogy at funeral of John Plantevigne, quoted in The Colored Harvest, Vol. VII (March 1913), 10.

bishop wrote Plantevigne that if he preached a mission[1] in New Orleans it "might stir up prejudices and suspicions calculated to endanger the real progress that I have just as much at heart as you have."[2] However, in 1913 and again in 1916, the archbishop permitted John Henry Dorsey, a black Josephite from Maryland, to preach at several black parishes.[3]

The entire priestly career of John Plantevigne was embarrassing to New Orleans church officials. Born in Pointe Coupée Parish, Plantevigne had attended college in New Orleans. Inspired by Janssens' favorable attitude toward black priests, he entered the Josephites, and was ordained in Baltimore. His return to his home parish and first Mass he celebrated there were observed with something less than the usual festive spirit. Father Louis Savoure, the pastor of Father Plantevigne's home parish in Chenel, Louisiana, advised extreme discretion due to what he felt was anti-black sentiment within the neighborhood. Consequently, Father Plantevigne offered his Mass on a weekday, quietly and without publicity. When he died in Baltimore in 1913 his family decided against having his body returned to Louisiana for burial. Several years earlier his brother, who had been active in civil rights work, was murdered and the family was afraid that the return of the priest's body to Chenel or Baton Rouge would cause further racial incidents.[4]

---

[1]A mission is a series of services in a parish usually conducted by a visiting priest and is designed to stimulate the faith of the parishioners.

[2]James Blenk, 31 March 1909, letter to John Plantevigne, quoted in its entirety in Foley, God's Men, pp. 87-88. Some New Orleans Negroes threatened to publicly expose the archbishop in the newspapers. Twenty years before they would not have hesitated, but in 1909 they made no public statement.

[3]The Colored Harvest, Vol. VII (June, 1913), 8; Vol. XII (June, 1916), 7.

[4]Foley, God's Men, pp. 81-84, 91.

The changing attitudes of the local and national hierarchy reflect the further waning of the status of blacks within the Church. Negroes had never ranked on equal terms with white Catholics but they had enjoyed a certain tolerance. Now, in New Orleans, they tended to be regarded as dependents of society who should be shunted off to mission parishes. The literary and scholastic attainments of the ante-bellum freemen of color were forgotten. Forgotten, too, were the days when the French priests of New Orleans considered Negroes as economic assets because of their generous contributions to the territorial churches.

These attitudes partially account for the most important aspect of the new separate parishes. They were virtually mandatory. Negroes automatically became members by virtue of their racial identification, and in no meaningful sense were they any longer free to remain affiliated with the territorial parishes. Since the chancery issued no public directive assigning Negroes to Jim Crow churches, it is impossible to give the exact date when the choice of attending either a territorial or a separate church, an option that Janssens had insisted on, was no longer available. In the city blacks remained on the parish register at the Cathedral and at some of the old French parishes. The latter, however, showed a definite drop in black baptisms after the erection of the black parish, Corpus Christi. When the black parishes of Blessed Sacrament, St. Dominic and Holy Ghost were formed, there was an immediate cessation of black baptisms in the neighboring territorial parishes.[1] Some Negroes in the new black parishes still attended Sunday Mass at their old parishes, but they were sent to the black churchs for weddings, funerals and baptisms.[2]

---

[1] New Orleans Archdiocesan Book of Parish Statistics, 1888-1918, New Orleans Archdiocesan Archives. Cited hereafter as Book of Parish Statistics.

[2] Catholics often fulfill Mass obligations at parishes other than their own, but church law requires

In contrast to the city, the change from choice to mandatory membership in Jim Crow parishes was more abrupt in the rural and small town areas. Lafayette's black parish, St. Paul's, was opened in 1912; after 1913 there were no further Negro baptism entries for the territorial parish. In 1911 a Josephite parish was formed at Napoleonville with an outmission at Klotzville. Black baptisms in the neighboring territorial parishes soon declined. No more black baptisms were recorded at Plattenville after 1911, at Paincourtville after 1912, and at Napoleonville after 1916.[1]

By 1918 the Jim Crow parish was commonplace in South Louisiana. Archbishop Blenk and other Church officials responsible for the establishment of segregated parishes probably believed that segregation, while bad in theory, was the only practical answer to the problems faced by the Church. As an institution in society, the Catholic Church affects and is affected by society. Sometimes it leads, sometimes it follows. In the racial field, the Church of South Louisiana elected to follow. When society chose Jim Crow, the Church, too, chose Jim Crow.

The members of the official church were not alone in their acceptance of separate churches. By the early 1900's some blacks were more willing to accept them. Sometimes they even requested separate churches, but not mandatory ones. Many blacks no longer saw any advantages in defiance or even protest. Some preferred to follow Booker T. Washington's admonitions to be patient in the face of discrimination. Several developments influenced the change in attitude. Jim Crow laws were multiplying, pushing Negroes more and more into a

---

them to be baptized, confirmed and married at the parish in which they are members. Therefore, sending Negroes to black parishes for weddings and other services meant that they were considered official members of the black parishes.

[1]Book of Parish Statistics.

ghetto environment where they became more dependent upon their own resources. Many of them believed that a hostile world forced them to rely on self-help and racial solidarity for survival. Contacts with the white community often decreased. Negro artisans who had depended upon the white trade gradually lost their position of power within the black community, as well as their financial security.[1]

In New Orleans the leaders who had opposed Jim Crowism were no longer vocal. The Negroes who had criticized the establishment of St. Katherine's parish were publicly silent when the other black parishes were formed in New Orleans. Their newspaper, The Daily Crusader, had suspended publication before 1900. Rather than censure the hierarchy, the existing Negro press in other sections of the country adopted a conciliatory attitude and at times praised Archbishop Blenk for his work among Louisiana Negroes.[2]

To many harrassed black Catholics, the Protestant faiths were visible proof that "separate but equal" churches had desirable qualities. They could not hope to have black priests, but in separate churches they could partially manage their own affairs. They would not have to worry about their own and their children's physical safety in an all black parish. The whites were antagonistic, especially in the rural areas, and some Negroes thought that the benefits obtained from integrated parishes were not worth the amount of discrimination they had to bear.

Blacks and whites from widely scattered parishes report that Negroes were not allowed to join parish

---

[1] Meier, Negro Thought in America, pp. 121-122, 139.

[2] The Colored Harvest, Vol. VIII (October, 1917), 10-11, quoted two black newspapers, The New York Age and The True Voice (Omaha), which praised Archbishop Blenk.

organizations like the Holy Name Society and the Sodality in the territorial parishes. Sometimes, of course, they did have their own benevolent societies. Black altar boys and choir members were unknown, and Catholic cemetaries often had segregated sections. In the church buildings blacks were placed in the more undesirable pews, in the back, to one side, or in a balcony. In one church a partition was built around the black pews. One Negro, who found himself at the end of the confession line after an hour of waiting, knew that the white people who edged him out of his place in line did not want him there at all. Negroes who dared to approach the communion rail before the whites had finished receiving were eased aside or advised not to repeat the action.[1]

Besides these humilating forms of discrimination, Negroes found themselves subject at times to physical attack. According to a black nun from Lafayette, the threat of physical violence was the reason for her family's support of separate parishes:

> My mother always said that she approved of the separate church because in the territorial church we sat in the back and seemed to have no part in anything. Furthermore, when they went to a mission at night for instance, the white boys threw flour on them or stuck them with hat pins or messed up their buggies. Nothing was done about it.[2]

Another incident in Lafayette further illustrates the increasing difficulties faced by black Catholics. Catholic schools were separate but the children attended joint

---

[1] Responses to questionnaires completed by twenty white and black Catholics of South Louisiana and Rev. M. L. Rousseve, S.V.D., letter to the editor, The Daily Advertiser (Lafayette), 1 May 1969. Copies of the questionnaires and general details about them are in the appendix.

[2] Questionnaire completed by Sister M. Jules, S.S.F.

catechism classes. The black children were advised by their parents not to fight back when they were bothered by the frequent harrassments of white children. On at least one occasion a small Negro did fight back. The girl struck a white boy who was bothering her, and they fell to the ground struggling. They were separated only after an adult intervened.[1] Such a response to bullying was rare; black children usually endured it.

Not all Negroes felt that the Church was promoting their best interests by furthering segregation. Many accepted separate parishes only reluctantly. However, the negative opinions were privately expressed. They were not recorded so that today they are very difficult to uncover. One statement may give an inkling to the undercurrent of disapproval. Frank Lapeyrolerie, of Reserve, Louisiana, commented on his family's hostility to a separate parish:

> It was easy for us to see that it was a step backwards since our parents had helped to build this beautiful brick building and with the separation of the congregation, the Negroes would have to go to a church built of wood. My parents disapproved and they thought that it was an injustice done to the Negroes.[2]

At least one Negro suspected the hierarchy of unchristian motives. "As far as I can see," remarked this person, "the bishop was prejudiced too."[3] Nevertheless, outwardly, blacks were much more docile and accommodating than they had been twenty years before.

---

[1] Mrs. Lillian LeBlanc Shay, personal interview with the author, 3 June 1965. Mrs. Shay was the small girl.

[2] Questionnaire completed by Frank Lapeyrolerie.

[3] Monsignor F. L. Gassler, 31 August 1941, letter to Roger Baudier, New Orleans Archdiocesan Archives.

Parish priests, too, adopted a more favorable attitude toward separate parishes. Many priests had to contend with growing congregations and crowded churches. Some white members were irritated when they could not rent a sufficient number of pews and Negro members were blamed for the problem.[1] Moreover, pastors needed additional assistants, but diocesan priests were in short supply. Various religious orders were willing to send priests to relieve the burdens of overworked pastors, but some of these orders were committed to working only with Negroes. Thus it was perhaps inevitable that pastors saw separate parishes as a solution to a number of their problems. They could reduce their congregations, lessen the possibility of racial incidents, and at the same time be assured that the black Catholics would receive adequate attention. By this time too, jurisdictional friction was no longer a problem. The Josephites had proven that they had no interest in whites, and that they would not lure them away from the territorial parishes.

Monsignor J. M. Langlois, of St. Peter's parish in New Iberia, was one pastor who requested a black parish. Archbishop Blenk invited the Holy Ghost Fathers to the town, and the Deed of Incorporation for St. Edward's, a black parish, was filed on December 12, 1917.[2] Some blacks were angry about the separate church, but eventually they submitted. Until November 10, 1918, when the church was dedicated, services were held in the territorial church. Father Xavier Lichtenberger, C. S. Sp., who was the pastor, was given permission to offer

---

[1] Monsignor F. L. Gassler, 31 August 1941, letter to Roger Baudier, New Orleans Archdiocesan Archives.

[2] Acts of Administration of Jules B. Jeanmard, Administrator, 20 April 1917 to 2 June 1918, New Orleans Archdiocesan Archives.

Sunday Mass at St. Peter's at a special time set aside for blacks.[1]

Developments at Thibodaux were fairly typical of other small town parishes. The separate church was not established until 1924, but plans were made several years before. Prior to 1915, Monsignor A. M. Barbier had discussed the project with the archbishop. Father LeBeau was to open the church at Thibodaux but he died in 1915. The next year the parish church was destroyed by fire and as a result the project was delayed.[2]

St. Paul's in Lafayette was the first small town parish which was built as a direct result of black requests for their own parish. In 1910 a Negro woman wrote to Archbishop Blenk and complained that Church officials always assumed that Negroes were happy and contented in the territorial parishes, but they never bothered to ask for their opinions. The archbishop contacted Father William Teurlings, who was at the time pastor of St. John's in Lafayette, and told him to investigate.

Teurlings was contacted at an opportune time, for he could easily acquire information about community sentiment at the many meetings which were being held to discuss a proposed new church for St. John's parish. At a meeting of one of the Negro benevolent societies he brought up the subject of separate parishes in an oblique manner:

> 'We are going to build a new church, as you know. Now is the time for you to talk, to say where you would like to be in the new church.' I watched their passive faces. 'Do you wish to be in the rear as you are now, or would you like to have an asile or a side

---

[1] St. Edward Parish Notes, New Orleans Archdiocesan Archives. Baudier, The Catholic Church in Louisiana, p. 516.

[2] St. Luke Parish Notes, signed by A. M. Barbier on 16 August 1923, New Orleans Archdiocesan Archives.

wing? Would you like to be upstairs or down? Give me your ideas so that I may serve you with consideration.¹

This choice of "black pews" was not very attractive to the Negroes and one of them finally told the pastor that they would prefer to build their own church. After further investigation, Father Teurlings concluded that most Lafayette Negroes desired a parish for themselves.

He then approached the whites to learn their opinion of separation:

> 'We are such a large congregation that we will have to build a church of huge proportions. Would it not be advisable and preferable and less expensive to build two churches, one for the whites and one for the colored?'²

The whites unanimously agreed, but they did not want the Negroes to reproach them for putting them out of the territorial parish. The mayor of Lafayette, who was a member of the congregation, believed the dilemma would be solved if the Negroes would only ask for a separate parish. When Father Teurlings explained that the Negroes had already asked for a church, the whites offered to show their goodwill by paying for it. The priest vetoed the idea and emphasized that the blacks should be responsible for building their own church. The fifteen hundred dollars they had contributed to the St. John's building fund was put into a fund for the new St. Paul's. Later it was used to buy the lot for the new church.³ The archbishop appointed Father Teurlings pastor

---

¹Teurlings, One Mile, p. 65.

²Ibid., p. 68.

³Ibid., pp. 67-68.

of St. Paul's, while he retained his position at St. John's. Such an arrangement was unique; St. Paul's was the only black parish established before 1918 under the direction of a diocesan priest. Father Teurlings remained pastor while the church was being built and the parish organized. Archbishop Blenk dedicated the church building on March 10, 1912. By 1914 the parish was functioning well, and Father Teurlings gave up his pastoral duties to the Holy Ghost Fathers.[1]

Many residents of Lafayette, especially laymen, saw St. Paul's as a final solution. Father Teurlings, however, viewed the parish as a temporary expedience and he suspected that Blenk, too, did not believe in permanent segregation. Teurlings noted that "the brilliant Archbishop, a man of keen vision, must have seen already in his day that separate churches could not be the final answer."[2] Yet, in the minds of such key figures as the archbishop, the black parishes had practical attractions that were hard to resist. Before the new parish of St. Paul's was on its feet in Lafayette, the Archbishop invited the Josephites into the Bayou Lafourche area to serve the needs of black Catholics living there. The mission complex consisted of Klotzville, Bertrandville and Bellrose. Eventually, the Josephites were to expand the mission parish to Plattenville, Paincourtville, and Napoleonville.[3]

On October 1, 1911, Father Benedict L. Favard opened the church which his parishioners later named St. Benedict's in honor of his patron saint. A few weeks later, on Christmas day, he celebrated his first Mass at

---

[1]The Morning Star (New Orleans), 15 July 1916. The Morning Star was the official diocesan newspaper of the Archdiocese of New Orleans.

[2]Teurlings, One Mile, p. 65.

[3]These towns are strung along the Bayou Lafourche in close proximity to each other. Bertrandville was about two miles from Napoleonville, and the address for St. Benedict's was Napoleonville.

the Klotzville church which had been neglected since the Assumptionists had quit the place. Father Favard described his first impressions of the building:

> The chapel is in awful state. There are about 14 glasses broken and when it rains, it rains from the altar to the front door. It is, I believe, too small, and the slightest storm will throw it down, for it is leaning on one side. The storm of 1908 partly demolished it, and they started to fix it again but never finished.[1]

Favard arranged for repairs at Klotzville and also reopened the school which had been closed for two years.

The next year Father Favard had to abandon his plans for a new church and school when the whole region was impoverished by a flood. In a report to his superior he described the havoc caused by the flood in his area:

> The current was so strong as to break over a mile of levee thus inundating several parishes or counties. All the crops are completely destroyed; no corn and especially no sugar cane. It will take 2 or 3 years to enable the planters to have any crop at all. The colored people who used to work on the plantations have no work to do any more and consequently no money. . . . The people were poor; they are still poorer now.[2]

---

[1] Father B. L. Favard, 26 December 1911, letter to Very Rev. Justin McCarthy, Superior, reprinted in The Colored Harvest, Vol. VI (March, 1912), 158.

[2] Father B. L. Favard, 15 June 1912, letter to Very Rev. Justin McCarthy, Superior, reprinted in The Colored Harvest, Vol. VI (October, 1912), 197.

As a result of the flood, the Josephites had extreme financial difficulties. Therefore, when St. Luke's was established at Thibodaux in 1924, the other Josephite parishes along the Lafourche were made its outmissions.[1]

In 1918, then, there were only four segregated parishes in the rural and small town areas of the archdiocese. The Josephites worked among the poorer Negroes at Petite Prairie and in the Bayou Lafourche region. The Holy Ghost Fathers were pastors among the more prosperous small town Negroes at St. Paul's parish in Lafayette and at St. Edward's parish in New Iberia. Although few in number, these parishes served as patterns for future segregated rural and small town parishes.

Archbishop Blenk's major efforts were not concentrated in the rural areas, however; but in New Orleans, where the number of separate parishes soon exceeded those in the country. In 1909 he asked the Josephites to establish the second black parish in New Orleans. As a result, St. Dominic's was established in the Carrolton area of the city.[2] It was a considerable distance from St. Katherine's, but it was not in the French district which had been so hostile to the Assumptionists. The popular Father LeBeau left Petite Prairie to become pastor. The territorial parish, Mater Dolorosa, had been moved to a new structure, and the Negroes were given the old church. Thus they did not have to raise money for a new building. Father LeBeau followed the usual pattern for an urban parish, opening a school, and forming numerous parish societies.[3]

---

[1] Baudier, The Catholic Church in Louisiana, p. 515.

[2] St. Dominic's was later renamed St. Joan of Arc.

[3] The Colored Harvest, Vol. VI (June, 1910), 44-45, and Baudier, The Catholic Church in Louisiana, p. 559. A new church was needed because the two parishes in Carrolton, St. Mary Nativity for the French and Mater Dolorosa for the Germans, were combined into one parish in 1898. Apparently the area needed two church, and instead of erecting another territorial parish, a black

Father LeBeau was energetic and won the support of many Negroes. The archbishop thought highly of him, and hoped that the Josephites would form more black parishes in New Orleans. But before 1915 the order had not committed itself to large scale parish work in New Orleans. This indecision prompted Church officials to search for another religious congregation which would be willing to work exclusively with blacks.[1] The Congregation of the Holy Ghost and the Immaculate Heart of Mary, commonly called the Holy Ghost Fathers, responded. This order had been at work for sometime in nearby dioceses. Bishop Cornelius Van de Ven had invited them to the Alexandria Diocese in 1911 and by 1914 they had organized several black parishes. They were also known for having founded black parishes in other Southern states.[2] The Holy Ghost Fathers did not normally confine themselves to black parishes. They were an international congregation which worked in the missions among people of all races. Nevertheless, the order agreed to the jurisdictional limitations demanded in New Orleans, and by 1918 the archbishop had given them charge of three black parishes in the Archdiocese of New Orleans. In 1914 they relieved the diocesan priests of duties at St. Paul's in Lafayette, and in 1917 they founded St. Edward's in New Iberia. The third parish was Holy Ghost in New Orleans. It was dedicated on October 7, 1916.

Katharine Drexel was largely responsible for the foundation of Holy Ghost parish. She appealed to Arch-

---

parish was formed. Negroes had been members of both the other parishes.

[1] F. L. Gassler, Vicar General of the Archdiocese of New Orleans, 10 September 1914, carbon copy of letter to Justin McCarthy, Josephite Superior, New Orleans Archdiocesan Archives. Cited hereafter as Gassler letter to McCarthy.

[2] Baudier, The Catholic Church in Louisiana, p. 504.

bishop Blenk to erect a new parish for blacks in the Louisiana Street area, and she requested that the Holy Ghost Fathers be in charge. She generously contributed $10,000 to the new parish.[1] Before giving the money to the archdiocese, she signed a contract with Church officials which specified that if the new parish building was ever sold all proceeds had to be used to continue work among Negroes. However, "if it be diverted... to any other purpose than for worship by and education in religion and secular knowledge of Colored People...,[2]" it would be returned to the Blessed Sacrament Sisters.

Still, the Josephites were considered the most desirable order, and diocesan officials were anxious that they send more priests to New Orleans. However, the Josephites had not been founded to run parishes for Negroes who lived in Catholic areas. Their primary reason for existence was to convert non-Christian and Protestant Negroes. After an understandable delay, during which they re-evaluated their goals, they agreed to manage urban parishes in New Orleans because of the lack of diocesan priests.[3] Understandable, too, was the impatience of Church officials who were awaiting the decision. The exasperated Vicar General finally wrote an outspoken letter to the Josephite superior pointing out that the Josephite system of caring for blacks was "absolutely faulty." He went on to explain that the

---

[1] The Morning Star (New Orleans), 6 April 1918, p. 3.

[2] Contract between Katharine Drexel and Archdiocese of New Orleans, copy in the Holy Ghost Fathers file, New Orleans Archdiocesan Archives.

[3] Peter E. Hogan, S.S.J., Josephite Archivist, 31 March 1965, letter to the author. Father Hogan writes, "...in theory we are not primarily 'Parish runners.' In practice, many if not most of our places are Parishes with a missionary purpose, the conversion of the American Negro as our goal. The running of parishes, purely as parishes, has evolved because of the shortages of priests in the United States, and particularly in southern dioceses."

order would have made New Orleans the center for all its missions, concentrating on Negro Catholics first, and then working among the Protestants.[1] The Josephites, however, did not take his advice. They remained faithful to their constitution, and most of their parishes were founded in Protestant areas of the South.

Nevertheless, they agreed to send more priests to New Orleans. The second Josephite parish in New Orleans, Blessed Sacrament, was dedicated at the same ceremonies as the new St. Francis Xavier High School on October 3, 1915. The state's black university, Southern, had been moved to Baton Rouge, and Father LeBeau persuaded Katharine Drexel to buy the old buildings for a Catholic high school. Archbishop Blenk readily gave his permission, and the property was purchased.[2] The Blessed Sacrament Sisters took charge of the school and later expanded it into a university.

Bishop J. M. Laval, Auxiliary of New Orleans, presided at the dedication in place of Archbishop Blenk who was ill. The ceremonies took place in the temporary Blessed Sacrament church, located in the auditorium of the school. In his address Bishop Laval pointed out the advantages of a separate parish, but made no mention of any liberty to attend the territorial parish. The main speaker, Father Alphonse Otis, S. J., president of Loyola University, stressed the importance of practical education for Negroes:

> It gives the thorough vocational training of which there is so much need in these days of specialized work. As to this special training, Booker Washington is my authority for the statement that if the Colored race is ever to come into its own, it will be through

---

[1] Gassler letter to McCarthy.

[2] *The Morning Star* (New Orleans), quoted in *The Colored Harvest*, Vol. VIII (January, 1916), 13-14.

industrial education. The Church realized
this long since, but was unable to give
what was needed.[1]

Some of the proud Creoles in the audience must have winced at the emphasis on manual education, but the discomfort caused by such remarks was undoubtedly outweighed by the satisfaction of having, at last, a Catholic high school that their children could attend.

In 1916 the Josephites ventured onto the edge of the old French area where the Assumptionists had been halted. The new Corpus Christi parish was situated in the heart of a section with a large Negro population, and immediately the priests were overwhelmed with parishioners. Father Samuel Kelly, S. S. J., had acquired two houses, one for a temporary church, the other for a rectory. After the dedication ceremonies of September 23, 1916, which drew several thousand blacks, Father Kelly realized that he needed a more spacious church. For a time he celebrated Sunday Mass in a nearby lot, while he hurriedly made plans for a church. Even before he could build a school, eight hundred children flocked to Sunday school, and during the first year one hundred and eighty persons were baptized. The parishioners welcomed a parish of their own and were willing to support it.[2]

In March, 1919, the church cornerstone was laid at an impressive ceremony. A multitude of black societies and bands marched with the priests and archbishop in a procession led by a group of aging veterans. These old men

---

[1] Ibid.

[2] The Colored Harvest, Vol. VIII (March, 1917), 6; The Colored Harvest, Vol. VIII (October, 1917), 3; The Colored Harvest, Vol. XXIX (February-March, 1942), 4. Corpus Christi was located in an area which was known for its devout and loyal black Catholics, before and during Archbishop Janssens' time and in the early days they had usually been treated well in the territorial churches. The reports that many of these people returned to the Church in 1916 are sad commentaries on the status of

could never have led a parade at a territorial parish in New Orleans, for they had served with the Union Army during the Civil War.[1] By October, 1919, when the new church was blessed, Corpus Christi was the largest Negro parish in the country. The new building was erected through the physical and financial efforts of the parishioners. Architect Louis Charbonnet volunteered his services without fee and designed the building, prepared the blueprints, and supervised the workers. Besides building the church, the men of the parish also made the altar, pews, and confessionals.[2]

The procession that preceded the blessing of the church that October day was even larger and grander than the previous one. The priests of the parish led the procession and were followed in order by "the First Communion classes, the parish organizations, the Corpus Christi Church Circles, the workingmen who built the church, the congregation in general, the Altar Society, societies of men, Holy Name Society, 1000 children of the parish, and the Knights of St. Peter Claver in uniform."[3] Numbering at least four thousand persons, they marched to the archbishop's residence on Esplanade Avenue where the archbishop joined the throng in a carriage and returned with them to the church for the blessing.

Negroes within the Church after 1900. It is foolish to assume that these people suddenly flocked to Protestant churches after so many years of loyalty to the Church. More likely, many of them had become disgusted with discrimination and simply stopped attending any church until the establishment of Corpus Christi.

[1]The Colored Harvest, Vol. IX (June, 1919), 3.

[2]The Colored Harvest, Vol. IX (January, 1920), 5.

[3]The Morning Star (New Orleans), quoted in ibid., 6.

No one can deny that the members of Corpus Christi parish were able to lead a full parochial life. Many Negroes returned to the practice of their Faith after the parish was begun, and the parishioners were proud of the new edifice, and on the surface seemed satisfied with the separate church arrangements. Any Church official, who viewed the developments of the parish, could well have concluded that segregated parishes were the ideal solution to the Church's racial problems.

Between 1909 and 1918 Janssens' experiment ceased to be an experiment; it had become a definite Church policy. The voluntary parishes had developed into Jim Crow parishes, accepted and praised by the official and non-official Church both white and black. Wide approval led to a rapid expansion of black parishes. By 1925 New Orleans had four more black parishes. By that year, too, rural and small town parishes had been started at Baton Rouge, Donaldsonville, New Roads, Crowley, Lake Charles, Opelousas, Breaux Bridge, Carencro, Rayne and Thibodaux. Jim Crow had indeed come to church.

85

EPILOGUE

Many more separate parishes were established after 1925, and as late as 1961 the Diocese of Lafayette formed two new segregated parishes. With the exception of St. Katherine's in New Orleans all of the separate parishes established before 1918 are still open.[1] Many small rural communities in the Diocese of Lafayette, which would have difficulty supporting one parish, can boast of two Catholic churches each with a small congregation. In several communities new church buildings were erected in black parishes in the 1960's giving the segregated arrangement added permanence.

The status of Negroes with respect to black parishes and the territorial parish within whose jurisdiction they reside remains substantially the same. Officially, membership is open to blacks in either the separate parish or the territorial parish in which they live. But Negroes generally understand that they are expected to worship at a black church, and it would be considered a rarity for a Negro to seek baptism, confirmation, matrimony, or a burial from a predominately white territorial church. Few, indeed, are the territorial parishes in which Negroes are welcome even for the more usual religious exercises. Many whites assume that there are "white" parishes and "black" parishes, and there are few official corrections of this assumption. If anything, official statements may have sometimes added to the confusion. In 1969, for instance, a spokesman for the Diocese of Lafayette publicly denied that discrimination was implied by separate parishes while admitting that Negroes were expected to be baptized, confirmed, and married at a black church. He referred to the efforts of black Catholics to obtain membership in "previously all-white parishes" even though "all-white" parishes

---

[1]St. Katherine's was closed as a parish in 1964 because it was in a downtown area and most of the congregation had moved away. A number of black parishes established later have also been closed.

have no official existence.[1]

It is not surprising then that few whites understand that there is no such thing as a "white" parish and that territorial parishes, in theory, are open to all Catholics who live within their territorial boundaries. In most rural areas of Southwest Louisiana it is a cause for parish-wide discussion when a black attends Sunday Mass in his territorial church. After one such incident a white parishoner posed a question that undoubtedly occurred to many others; "Since they have their own church," the parishoner asked, "why should they come to ours?"

At this writing in mid-1971 there is some evidence of movement toward re-integration of parishes in Southwest Louisiana. The Diocese of Lafayette has formulated a definite policy against establishing any new segregated parishes. Several new territorial parishes have been created to serve congregations which are mainly black and they are staffed by diocesan priests. On the other hand, this diocese which contains the great majority of segregated parishes in Louisiana, has done little to put an end to the existing pattern of segregation.

In sharp contrast the Archdiocese of New Orleans besides having a firm policy against the establishment of new segregated parishes, also has a definite policy of fostering integration in present church parishes. The Archdiocese in 1965 had fewer than ten black parishes outside the city of New Orleans. In the past few years four of these parishes have merged with the

---

[1] Rev. Robert Landry, Diocesan Director of Press and Information, quoted in "Action Corner," The Daily Advertiser (Lafayette), 26 April 1969. In contrast the Archdiocese of New Orleans does not expect Negroes to use a black parish. Archbishop Philip M. Hannan writes, "We encourage blacks to attend the territorial parish in which they live," Philip M. Hannan, Archbishop, Archdiocese of New Orleans, letter, 23 June 1971, to the author.

local territorial parishes. Meetings were called to prepare all parishioners for the change and to welcome black Catholics to the territorial parishes.

In New Orleans, itself, one black parish was discontinued after a hurricane destroyed the church building. Members now attend nearby territorial parishes. Another former black parish has taken over the territorial boundaries of a predominately white parish. The church of the latter parish is now a shrine and all records are kept at the former black parish. Furthermore, in New Orleans three former black parishes have been designated territorial parishes.[1] New Orleans thus seems to be making progress in its efforts to do away with mandatory segregated parishes.

It is the Diocese of Lafayette which presently faces the greatest problems with the existing segregated parishes. A number of familiar factors are at work today which impede efforts aimed at re-integrating Catholics in their churches.

Financial factors undoubtedly add to the permanence of the segregated status quo. If territorial parishes are re-integrated, it may be expected that some of the money received from the annual collection for the Indian and Negro missions will be sent to other dioceses. The physical plants that make up present black parishes represent a considerable capital expense and they undoubtedly lend a certain degree of "staying power" to separate parishes.[2]

---

[1] Archbishop Philip M. Hannan letter, 23 June 1971.

[2] Ibid. Several black parishes in New Orleans with substantial church buildings are located two blocks from territorial churches. It is not practical to close down the church itself and it is almost impossible to assign separate territorial boundaries to parishes that are so close together.

Then, too, there is a scarcity of priests in South Louisiana, and the question of whether the re-integration of territorial parishes in a particular diocese will result in the loss of priests is yet unanswered. The dioceses of South Louisiana have had to rely on religious orders to alleviate the shortage of priests, but in some cases orders have sent priests to the area primarily, and even exclusively, for the purpose of staffing black parishes. Today only a few diocesan priests are pastors of black parishes. The Josephites and the Holy Ghost Fathers have been joined by the priests of the Society of the Divine Word. The latter order has stressed the development of a local clergy and many of their priests are black, but, like the other orders, they are not committed only to South Louisiana. Negro priests in South Louisiana, most of whom are members of the Society of the Divine Word, are concentrated in the Diocese of Lafayette where they are pastors of about a quarter of the black parishes.

Naturally, any bishop would be reluctant to lose the services of a large number of his priests, and the question of whether a significant number of priests would leave South Louisiana if black parishes were closed is a crucial one. When this question was asked of Father Peter E. Hogan, the Archivist of the Josephite Order, which staffs a great number of the black parishes, he could not give a conclusive reply:

> My most definite answer would be: 'I don't know.' On the basis of presumption I will try to answer in more detail....The implication is not quite accurate to say that we are only premitted to work with Negroes. It seems better to say that the purpose of our existence, the reason for our foundation, the reason for which men join our community, is to dedicate themselves to the Negro race. Hence, if there were a full integration of parishes in Louisiana, I suppose we would stay on as pastors only in those places where the parishes were largely in Negro areas,

and there were not sufficient diocesan or other priests to supply our places. We might well want to remain in the dioceses for new approaches towards the conversion of the Negro race, by convert centers or any other means that might be effective.[1]

Another major factor impeding the abandonment of black parishes is the hostility of whites to re-integration. It is ultimately this hostility that lies at the base of the argument, often made by diocesan officials, that most blacks prefer to maintain separate parishes rather than risk losing the positions they now enjoy in black parishes. They express the fear that if black parishes are abandoned many blacks will abandon the Church and become Protestants. Concerned Negroes have pointed out, sometimes in face to face confrontations with the highest diocesan officials, that such attitudes are essentially paternalistic and are based on scanty information and under-estimation of the leadership potential of the hierarchy in this policy area. They argue that there is much greater diversity of opinion among Negroes than some officials realize.

The destruction by fire in December, 1970 of a black parish church structure in the Diocese of Lafayette provided an opportunity to observe the attitudes of black parishioners concerning separate parishes. It was readily apparent that there was in fact a wide diversity of opinion regarding the question of whether the parish church should be rebuilt and the separate parish continued. By no means did all the parishioners favor the separate parish. One group of parishioners, comprised mainly of officers of the parish organizations and other parish leaders, strongly maintained that the church should not be rebuilt and that to do so would only add permanence to an unchristian arrangement. A

---

[1] Father Peter E. Hogan, Josephite Archivist, letter of 31 March 1965 to the author.

second group argued that the separate parish should be continued as a necessary means of maintaining and developing black racial identity. A third group, consisting largely of older parishioners, feared that whites in a territorial parish might not accept their presence and they did not care to be treated in an unchristian way in church. A final group, probably the largest of all, appeared to be apathetic toward the problem and was generally prepared to accept any arrangement. Reportedly, plans are being discussed to replace the burned out church with a small transitional structure in which services will be held for those blacks who insist on a separate church. Apparently most of the congregation will attend the territorial parish in which all parish records will most likely be kept.

In the questionnaires referred to in earlier chapters, Negroes living in widely scattered areas of South Louisiana expressed a good deal of dissatisfaction with mandatory separate parishes.[1] An optimistic nun wrote that separate churches are no longer needed because "both races are better educated than in the past." A Lafayette housewife believed that separate churches hurt the unity of the Catholic Church. She believed that the Church "should always have been and still be One. This is the way all true Christians should feel." A black businessman brought up the doctrine of the Mystical Body. Separate parishes, he pointed out, do little to encourage belief in that doctrine, which maintains that all Christians are spiritually bound together. One Negro observed that although separate churches are not good, they will most likely be continued because "white people have not yet learned enough religion to accept Negroes anyhow."

The last response is further evidence of a major difficulty encountered by plans for re-integration which

---

[1] Moreover, the author taught for three years at a black Catholic high school in Lafayette, Louisiana, and during that time she never met any Negro who approved of mandatory segregated parishes.

was mentioned earlier--the confusion and hostility among white Catholics. In her sample of opinion of white Catholics in South Louisiana, the author did not encounter many respondents whose attitudes favored re-integration. Nevertheless, the responses often lent support to the argument of some black leaders that the present position of the official Church is based on an under-estimation of its leadership potential. Most white Catholics who responded to the author's questionnaire indicated their willingness to obey the instructions of the bishop. "I believe in segregation and have always practiced segregation," stated one man. "I believe it will prevent mongrelization of the races." Yet he added that if the parishes were re-integrated, "I would abide by the bishop's decision even if I would not approve of it." One woman wrote that she would continue to practice her religion if blacks came to her parish church, but she made it clear that she "would make it my business not to sit near one if possible." Another woman observed that "mixing the races can do no good and will probably do harm." However, she will "accept the ruling of the bishop." A high school teacher indicated that one of the best reasons for maintaining separate parishes was to protect the older Negroes who are "not too well educated" and who would "likely be hurt by those whites who are very prejudiced."

Some whites in the area have taken definite stands in favor of re-integration. A number of white priests have been outspoken in their condemnation of mandatory segregated parishes for moral reasons. An increasing number of laymen, too, have begun to question the continuance of Jim Crow parishes in South Louisiana. One resident of Lafayette, in a letter to the local newspaper, held that segregated parishes are patently unchristian. He added, "It is long since time that Christian churches practiced Christianity in race relations. It is time Christians labeled mandatory segregation and discrimination as immoral regardless of the excuses put forward to defend them."[1]

The bishops have made a number of statements regarding racial justice, but the majority of black Catholics in Louisiana remain members of mandatory segregated parishes. In Southwest Louisiana, Catholic segregationists have good reason to believe that they can rely upon the Church to be the last bulwark of segregation. They know that they may be forced to sit next to a Negro on a bus, or they might find one at the next table in a restaurant. However, they can find a haven in their parish church as they will not likely find a Negro in the next pew. Certainly, the experiment of the 1890's has become the dilemma of the 1970's. Louisiana bishops, although cautious on the surface, have undoubtedly been as concerned with the current problems as Archbishop Janssens was with the old one. Archbishop Philip M. Hannan of New Orleans has shown proof of this concern by taking definite action toward re-integrating parishes in his jurisdiction. Recent developments may be a sign that future historians will be able to refer to the decade of the 1970's as the period when there was a movement to re-integrate all parishes of South Louisiana.

---

[1] The Daily Advertiser, 1 May 1969, Robert R. Jones, letter to the editor.

APPENDIX

QUESTIONNAIRE ON SEPARATE CHURCHES IN SOUTH LOUISIANA

Twenty white and Negro Catholics, who remember the early separate parishes, completed the questionnaires. The questionnaires were used to acquire anecdotes and opinions from members of the non-official Church, whom the author did not contact personally. No attempt was made to compile objective statistics from the material received. The questionnaires were returned by Catholics who live in New Orleans, Lafayette, Maurice, Reserve, Donaldsonville, Church Point, Rayne, New Iberia, Grand Coteau, Kaplan, Breaux Bridge, Franklin and Carencro.

<u>Questionnaire sent to Negroes</u>:

1-Where were you born? What year?
2-What church and town were you baptized in?
3-Was there a school for Negroes connected to your parish? Did you attend it?
4-What parish did you belong to at the time a Negro parish was started in your area?
5-Could you sit in any part of the church you desired in that parish, or were certain seats reserved for you? If certain seats were reserved, were they on one side, or in the back of the church?
6-If you continued to attend your old parish church after a Negro parish was started in your area, were you welcome or did the parishioners and priests encourage you to attend the Negro church?
7-Did you approve or disapprove when you heard that a separate parish would be started for Negroes in your area? Why did you feel the way you did? Do you remember what your parents thought about the separate parish?
8-Why do you think the Bishop decided to build separate churches for Negroes?

9-In the old parish could you belong to parish organizations such as the Holy Name Society or Sodality? Were Negroes allowed in the choir? Were Negroes allowed to be altar boys?
10-Did the old parish have a cemetary? Were there separate sections for the two races?
11-In your old parish did the white parishioners ever show that they were happy to have you in that parish? If so, how?
12-In your old parish did the white parishioners ever show that they did not want you in that parish? If so, how?
13-Do you think that it is a good idea to have separate parishes for the races today? Why or why not?

Questionnaire sent to whites:

1-Where were you born? What year?
2-What parish and town were you baptized in? If you have not always belonged to that parish, what parish did you belong to when a Negro parish was started in your area?
3-Before there were separate churches for Negroes and white Catholics what did you think about Negroes attending the same church as white people?
4-Did you approve or disapprove when you heard that a separate church would be started for Negroes? Why did you think the way you did?
5-When was the first Negro parish started in your area? What was the name of it? Did any Negroes keep coming to your church after a parish was started for them?
6-Why do you think the Bishop decided to build separate churches for Negroes?
7-Before the Negro parish was built, could Negroes belong to parish organizations such as the Holy Name Society and Sodality? Were Negroes allowed in the choir? As altar boys?
8-Was a special section of the church set aside for Negroes, or could they sit where they wished? If there were separate pews, were they on one side or in the back of the church? Was there a special section of the Communion rail reserved for Negroes?

9-What did your pastor think about having Negroes attend the same church with whites?
10-Do you think that it is a good idea to have separate parishes for the races today? Why or why not? What would you do if the Bishop announced that next Sunday both races were to go to the same churches, and that there would not be any more separate churches?

BIBLIOGRAPHY

I. ARCHIVES

NEW ORLEANS ARCHDIOCESAN ARCHIVES

Ante-Bellum files.

Correspondence of Chancery officials.

Correspondence of Archbishops Francis Xavier Leray, Francis Janssens and James Blenk.

Janssens, Francis, Diary, 1889-1895.

Parish Records from St. Rose de Lima and St. Katherine of New Orleans, St. Luke of Thibodaux and St. Edward of New Iberia.

Parish Statistics, 1888-1918, New Orleans Archdiocesan Book of Religious Orders, Files of the Assumptionists, Josephites and Holy Ghost Fathers.

JOSEPHITE ARCHIVES

Benoit, Canon Peter L., Diary of a Trip to America, January 6, 1875 to June 8, 1875, III Volumes, original in Mill Hill Fathers Archives.

The Colored Harvest.

St. Joseph's Advocate.

II. PERSONAL CORRESPONDENCE

Hogan, Rev. Peter E., Josephite Archivist, four letters, March-June, 1965, to the author.

Tennelly, Rev. J. B., Secretary, Commission for the Catholic Mission among the Colored People and the Indians,

March 3, 1965, to the author.

Rareshide, Rev. Lanaux, Assistant Chancellor, Archdiocese of New Orleans, January 22, 1971, to the author.

III. INTERVIEWS

Iverson, Rev. Stanley J., Vice Chancellor, Archdiocese of New Orleans, personal interview, New Orleans, 11 March 1965.

Shay, Mrs. Lilliam LeBlanc, personal interview, Lafayette, Louisiana, 3 June 1965.

Sister Francis Regis, S.S.F., Principal, Holy Rosary Institute, Lafayette, Louisiana, personal interview, 1 December 1970.

Speyrer, Msgr. Jude, Pastor, Our Lady Queen of Peach Parish, Lafayette, Louisiana, personal interview, 12 January 1971.

IV. NEWSPAPERS

New Orleans, The Telegraph/ Le Telegraphe.

New Orleans, The Daily Picayune.

New Orleans, The Morning Star.

New Orleans, The Times-Democrat.

Lafayette, The Daily Advertiser.

V. BOOKS

Acts Passed at the Second Session of the Sixth Legislature of the State of Louisiana, New Orleans, 1824.

Baudier, Roger, The Catholic Church in Louisiana, New Orleans, 1939.

Ellis, John Tracy, American Catholicism, Chicago, 1956.

Ezell, John Samuel, The South since 1865, New York, 1963.

Fichter, Joseph H., Dynamics of a City Parish, Vol. I of Southern Parish, Chicago, 1951.

Foley, Albert Sidney, God's Men of Color: The Colored Catholic Priests of the United States, 1854-1954, New York, 1955.

Franklin, John Hope, From Slavery to Freedom: A History of American Negroes, New York, 1947.

Frazier, E. Franklin, The Negro in the United States, New York, 1957.

Gillard, John Thomas, Colored Catholics in the United States, Baltimore, 1941.

Jordon, Winthrop D., White Over Black: American Attitudes toward the Negro, 1550-1812, Chapel Hill, 1968.

McConnell, Roland C., Negro Troops of Ante-bellum Louisiana: A History of the Battalion of Freemen of Color, Baton Rouge, 1968.

Meier, August, Negro Thought in America, 1880-1915: Racial Ideologies in the Age of Booker T. Washington, Anne Arbor, 1963.

Rahner, Hugo, editor, The Parish, translator, Robert Kress, Westminster, Maryland, 1958.

Rousseve, Charles B., The Negro in Louisiana, New Orleans, 1937.

Simkins, Francis Butler, A History of the South, New York, 1953.

Sweet, William Warren, Methodism in American History, Nashville, (Revision of 1953), 1961.

Teurlings, William, One Mile an Hour, adapted by Rosalind Foley, New York, 1959.

Woodson, Carter G., The History of the Negro Church, Washington, 1921.

_____. Free Negro Heads of Families in the United States in 1830, Washington, 1925.

VI. ARTICLES AND PAMPHLETS

Dethloff, Henry C. and Robert R. Jones, "Race Relations in Louisiana, 1877-98," Louisiana History, IX (Fall 1968), 301-323.

Everett, Donald E., "Free Persons of Color in Colonial Louisiana," Louisiana History, VII (Winter 1966), 21-51.

Guste, Robert, "For Men of Goodwill," New Orleans, 1957.

Kunkel, Paul A., "Modifications in Louisiana Negro Legal Status under Louisiana Constitutions, 1812-1957," Journal of Negro History, XLIV (January 1959), 1-26.

Nelson, Alice Dunbar, "People of Color in Louisiana," Journal of Negro History, I (October 1916), 361-376 and II (January 1917), 51-78.

Reinders, Robert C., "The Decline of the New Orleans Free Negro in the Decade before the Civil War," Journal of Mississippi History, XXIV (April 1962), 88-98.

_____. "The Free Negro in the New Orleans Economy, 1850-1860," Louisiana History, VI (Summer 1965), 273-286.

Reinders, Robert C., "Churches and the Negro in New Orleans, 1850-1860," *Phylon*, XXII (Fall 1961), 241-248.

Riddell, William Renwick, "Le Code Noir," *Journal of Negro History*, X (July 1925), 321-329.

Stahl, Annie, "The Free Negro in Ante-Bellum Louisiana," *Louisiana Historical Quarterly*, XXV (April 1942), 301-397.

INDEX

African Methodist Church, 49
Aitken, Mamie Power, 52
Albert, John, 64
Alexandria, Diocese of, 79
Allain, Mme. Frédéric, 10
Altar Society, 83
American Ecclesiastical
 Review, 30
Assumptionist Contract, 44-46
Assumptionist Fathers, 39,
 42-49,56,57,77,82
Austin, Mother, 20

Baltimore, Plenary Council
 of, 20-22
Barbier, A. M., 74
Barnabe, Father, 56
Baton Rouge, 23,58,67,81,84
Baudier, Roger, 3
Bayou Lafourche, 76,78
Bellrose, La.,
Benoit, Peter L., 17
Bertrandville, La., 76
Bienville, 8
Blanc, Antoine, 33
Blenk, James Hubert, 63,64,
 66,67,69,70,73,74,76,78,
 80,81
Blessed Sacrament Church, 81
Blessed Sacrament Parish, 68,
 81
Blessed Sacrament Sisters,
 80,81
Black Code, Spanish, 8
Bogaerts, J. B., 56,57
Bois Mallet, 3
Breaux Bridge, 84

Cabrini, Frances Xavier, 30
Carencro, La., 84

Chapelle, Louis Placide,
 27,57,63
Charbonnet, Louis, 83
Chassé, L. A., 19
Chenel, La., 67
Citizens' Committee, 54
Civil Code, 10
Civil War, 1,15,17,18,
 21,23,32,83
Code Noir, 8
The Colored Harvest, 31,
 41,47,59-61,64,66,67,
 70,77,78,81-83
Commission for Catholic
 Missions Among the Colored People and Indians
 19,22,34,35,53
Comité des Citoyens, 53
Corpus Christi Church
 Circles, 83
Corpus Christi Parish,
 68,82-84
Creoles, 18
Crowley, La., 84
Cuddy, Peter, 56

Daily Advertiser, The,
 71,86,91
Daily Crusader, The, 54,
 70
Daily Picayune, 13,52,55
Decuire, Antoine, 12
Deslondes, Victoire, 12
Dethloff, Henry C., 4
Donaldsonville, La., 10
Dorsey, John H., 65,67
Drexel, Katharine, 25,39,
 46,51,79-81

Elder, William H., 39-40
Ellis, John T., 21

Emancipation Proclamation, 15
English Mill Hill Fathers, 17
Ezell, John S., 1
Everett, Donald E., 11

Favard, Benedict L., 76,77
Fichter, Joseph H., 5
Fleming, Walter, L, 3
Foley, Albert S., 64
Franklin, John H., 3
Free People of Color, 11-15

Gassler, F. L., 36,37,72, 73,79,81
Gens de Couleur, 11,12
Gibbons, James, 64-66
Gillard, John T., 15
Greene, Father, 32
Guste, Robert, 1

Hogan, Peter E., 24,65,80, 87,88
Holy Ghost Fathers, 73,76, 78-80,87
Holy Ghost Parish, 68,79
Holy Name Society, 71,83
Homeyer, J., 7

Immaculate Conception Parish, 31,60,61
Iverson, Sanley J., 6

Janssens, Francis, 25,27-35,37-43,46-51,53-59, 62-66,68,82,84
Jeanmard, Jule B., 73
Jefferson College, 63
Jesuits, 9
Jones, Robert R., 4
Jordan, Winthrop D., 9

Josephites, 17,24,25, 31,32,58-60,62,64, 65,67,69,71,73,76-82,87
Jules, Sister M., 71

Kelly, Samuel, 82
Klotzville, La., 46-49, 57,69,76,77
Knights of St. Peter Claver, 83
Kunkel, Paul, 10
Lafayette, La., 25,37, 69,71,74-76,78,79,89, 90
Lafayette, Diocese of, 4, 85-87
Lake Charles, La., 84
Landry, Pierre, 10
Landry, Robert, 86
Lapeyrolerie, Frank, 72
Laval, J. M., 81
LeBeau, Pierre O., 59-62,74,78,79
Leo XIII, 25
Leray, Francis Xavier, 18,23
Les Artisans, 12
Les Censelles, 12
Lesaichere, Jean Baptiste, 47,48
Lichtenberger, Xavier, 73
Loyola University, 81

McCarthy, Justin, 77,79, 81
McConnell, Roland C., 12
Maistre, Claude, 15,16
Marcellin, Father, 42,43, 46,47,56
Massardier, J. N., 57
Matre Dolorosa, 78

Mathis, Father, 9
Mercy, Sisters of, 19,20
Mill Hill Fathers, 17,25
Morning Star, The, 76,80, 81,83

Napoleonville, La., 69, 76
Natchez, Miss., 28
Natchitoches Parish, La., 11
Nelson, Alice D. 11
New Iberia, La., 25,78, 79
New Orleans, Archdiocese of, 2,20,23,24,27,40, 64,86
New Orleans, First Black Parish in, 3
New Roads, La., 84
New York Age, The, 70
Notre Dame du Sacre Coeur, Pastor of, 57
Nugent, F. V., 51

Odin, Jean Marie, 6, 16
"Old Willing Workers," 56
Opelousas, La., 37,84
Otis, Alphonse, 81

Paincourtville, La., 42, 45-48,57,69,76
Palmetto, La., 58,59
Perche, Napoleon, 15,17, 23
Petite Prairie, La., 31, 35,59-62,78
Plantevigne, John, 66,67
Plattenville, La., 69,76
Pointe Coupée Parish, La., 11,12,60,67
Port Barre, La., 59,60

Rareshide, Lanaux J., 6,86
Raymond, Gilbert, 18
Rayne, La., 84
Reconstruction, 2
Reinders, Robert C., 12,49
Renaudier, F. L., 42,46
Reserve, La., 72
Revolution, American, 9
Richmond, Diocese of, 28
Riddle, William R., 8
Rousseve, Charles B., 9

St. Ann, Pastor of, 57
St. Augustine Parish, 14
St. Augustine, Pastor of, 57
St. Benedict church, 76
St. Boniface, Pastor of, 57
St. Dominic Parish, 68,78
St. Edward Parish, 25,73, 78,79
St. Francis Xavier High School, 81
St. Francis Xavier Parish (Baltimore), 24
St. John the Baptist Parish, La., 12
St. John church, 74-76
St. John Parish, 15
St. Joseph church, 53,54
St. Joseph Parish, 23,51
St. Joseph, Society of (See Josephites)
St. Katherine Parish, 25, 52-56,62,70,78,85
St. Landry Parish, La., 11
St. Louis church, 14
St. Luke Parish, 78
St. Martin Parish, La., 11
St. Martinville, La., 37
St. Paul Church, 74-76
St. Paul Parish, 25,69,74, 78,79

St. Rose de Lima Parish, 15,16
St. Rose de Lima, Pastor of, 57
Sacred Heart, Religious of, 19,20
Sanctuary Society, 52
Santo Domingo, 11, 24
Savoure, Louis, 67
Schwer, W., 33
Shay, Lillian LeBlanc, 72
Simkins, Francis B., 1,3
Sisters of the Blessed Sacrament for Indians and Colored People, 25
Slattery, J. R., 58,59,61, 65
Slave Codes, 8
"The Society for a Good Death," 48
Society of the Divine Word, 87
Sodality, The, 71
Stahl, Annie, 11
Starr, Monsignor, 65
Superior Council of La., 9
Sweet, William W, 3

Taylor, Joe Gray, 14
The Telegraph/La Telegraphe, 13
Teurlings, William 35,36, 74-76
Texas and Pacific Railroad, 61
Thibodaux, La., 74,78,84
Tillard, John T., 53
Times-Democrat, 39,51
Trent, Council of, 6
True Voice, The, 70

Ven, Cornelius Van de, 79
Vincentians, 51,55,56

Washington, La., 59,60
Washington, Booker T., 69,81
Woodson, Carter S., 3,11

THE AMERICAN CATHOLIC TRADITION

An Arno Press Collection

Callahan, Nelson J., editor. **The Diary of Richard L. Burtsell, Priest of New York.** 1978

Curran, Robert Emmett. **Michael Augustine Corrigan and the Shaping of Conservative Catholicism in America, 1878-1902.** 1978

Ewens, Mary. **The Role of the Nun in Nineteenth-Century America** (Doctoral Thesis, The University of Minnesota, 1971). 1978

McNeal, Patricia F. **The American Catholic Peace Movement 1928-1972** (Doctoral Dissertation, Temple University, 1974). 1978

Meiring, Bernard Julius. **Educational Aspects of the Legislation of the Councils of Baltimore, 1829-1884** (Doctoral Dissertation, University of California, Berkeley, 1963). 1978

Murnion, Philip J., **The Catholic Priest and the Changing Structure of Pastoral Ministry, New York, 1920-1970** (Doctoral Dissertation, Columbia University, 1972). 1978

White, James A., **The Era of Good Intentions: A Survey of American Catholics' Writing Between the Years 1880-1915** (Doctoral Thesis, University of Notre Dame, 1957). 1978

Dyrud, Keith P., Michael Novak and Rudolph J. Vecoli, editors. **The Other Catholics.** 1978

Gleason, Philip, editor. **Documentary Reports on Early American Catholicism.** 1978

Bugg, Lelia Hardin, editor. **The People of Our Parish.** 1900

Cadden, John Paul. **The Historiography of the American Catholic Church: 1785-1943.** 1944

Caruso, Joseph. **The Priest.** 1956

Congress of Colored Catholics of the United States. **Three Catholic Afro-American Congresses.** [1893]

Day, Dorothy. **From Union Square to Rome.** 1940

Deshon, George. **Guide for Catholic Young Women.** 1897

Dorsey, Anna H[anson]. **The Flemmings.** [1869]

Egan, Maurice Francis. **The Disappearance of John Longworthy.** 1890

Ellard, Gerald. **Christian Life and Worship.** 1948

England, John. **The Works of the Right Rev. John England, First Bishop of Charleston.** 1849. 5 vols.

Fichter, Joseph H. **Dynamics of a City Church.** 1951
Furfey, Paul Hanly. **Fire on the Earth.** 1936
Garraghan, Gilbert J. **The Jesuits of the Middle United States.** 1938. 3 vols.
Gibbons, James. **The Faith of Our Fathers.** 1877
Hecker, I[saac] T[homas]. **Questions of the Soul.** 1855
Houtart, François. **Aspects Sociologiques Du Catholicisme Américain.** 1957
[Hughes, William H.] **Souvenir Volume. Three Great Events in the History of the Catholic Church in the United States.** 1889
[Huntington, Jedediah Vincent]. **Alban: A Tale of the New World.** 1851
Kelley, Francis C., editor. The First American Catholic Missionary Congress. 1909
Labbé, Dolores Egger. **Jim Crow Comes to Church.** 1971
LaFarge, John. **Interracial Justice.** 1937
Malone, Sylvester L. **Dr. Edward McGlynn.** 1918
The Mission-Book of the Congregation of the Most Holy Redeemer. 1862
O'Hara, Edwin V. **The Church and the Country Community.** 1927
Pise, Charles Constantine. **Father Rowland.** 1829
Ryan, Alvan S., editor. **The Brownson Reader.** 1955
Ryan, John A., **Distributive Justice.** 1916
Sadlier, [Mary Anne]. **Confessions of an Apostate.** 1903
Sermons Preached at the Church of St. Paul the Apostle, New York, During the Year 1863. 1864
Shea, John Gilmary. **A History of the Catholic Church Within the Limits of the United States.** 1886/1888/1890/1892. 4 Vols.
Shuster, George N. **The Catholic Spirit in America.** 1928
Spalding, J[ohn] L[ancaster]. **The Religious Mission of the Irish People and Catholic Colonization.** 1880
Sullivan, Richard. **Summer After Summer.** 1942
[Sullivan, William L.] **The Priest.** 1911
Thorp, Willard. **Catholic Novelists in Defense of Their Faith, 1829-1865.** 1968
Tincker, Mary Agnes. **San Salvador.** 1892
Weninger, Franz Xaver. **Die Heilige Mission** *and* **Praktische Winke Für Missionare.** 1885. 2 Vols. in 1
Wissel, Joseph. **The Redemptorist on the American Missions.** 1920. 3 Vols. in 2
The World's Columbian Catholic Congresses and Educational Exhibit. 1893
Zahm, J[ohn] A[ugustine]. **Evolution and Dogma.** 1896